THE RIGHTS
OF
THE VICTIM

THE RIGHTS OF THE VICTIM

BY MARGARET O. HYDE

Franklin Watts

New York / London / Toronto / Sydney

1983

Library of Congress Cataloging in Publication Data

Hyde, Margaret Oldroyd, 1917-
The rights of the victim.

Bibliography: p.
Includes index.
Summary: Discusses violent crime and its victims,
including how to understand and help victims
and how to reduce the risk of becoming one.
1. Victims of crimes—United States
—Juvenile literature. 2. Victims of crimes
—Services for—United States
—Juvenile literature. [1. Victims of crimes.
2. Crimes and criminals] I. Title.
HV6250.3.U5H92 1983   362.8′8′0973   82-17610
ISBN 0-531-04596-X

To Carol Wazrek Reichard
and
Harry Clinton Reichard, D.V.M.

CONTENTS

1
Who Are the Victims?
1

2
From Blood Feuds to the Justice of Today
13

3
The Criminal and the Victim
23

4
Understanding the Victim
33

5
How to Help a Crime Victim
47

6
Services for Victims
55

7
Toward Justice for Victims
65

8
Reducing the Risk of Becoming a Victim
79

Suggestions for Further Reading
93

Sources of Further Information
97

*Directory of Offices of
State Crime Victim Compensation*
101

Glossary
107

Index
111

THE RIGHTS
OF
THE VICTIM

1

WHO ARE
THE VICTIMS?

Will you be one of the fifty-seven million people who may become victims of crime this year? If you are not directly victimized by burglary, rape, or some other crime, you may be a victim who suffers indirectly from the agony of a relative or friend. In the broadest sense, everyone is a victim of crime. The hidden costs of crime include fear, grief, and other emotional problems, as well as the costs to citizens of maintaining the whole criminal justice system.

In America at present, the state takes little or no responsibility for the welfare of the persons most directly affected by crime—the victims themselves. Although a major role of government is the protection of its citizens, the criminal justice system is oriented to the rights of the accused.

A common dictionary definition of a victim reads in part as follows: "Someone who is deceived or cheated by his own emotions, by the dishonesty of others, or by some impersonal force." There are many different kinds of victims: victims of dishonesty or crimes of violence, victims of an impersonal force such as war or epidemic, victims of accident or catastrophe. In all cases, the victim is a sufferer.

But people react differently to different kinds of victims. For example, the victims of accidents or natural forces such as floods and hurricanes evoke sympathy, but victims of crime tend to be ignored or even shunned. Regardless of circumstances, victims may be thought of as helpless or weak. The interaction between the criminal and the victim is seen as a win-lose situation with the victim stigmatized as a loser. Or victims may be viewed as deserving their fate—as having somehow "brought it on themselves." Rape victims are often viewed in this way, even when the victim has had no previous contact with the rapist before the crime.

There are cases in which a victim plays a part in what happens to him or her. However, for the most part, victims are the innocent and neglected element in the criminal justice system. With the exception of famous or handicapped persons, emphasis in the media, as in the criminal justice system, is on the crime and the criminal rather than the victim.

However, in some areas, attitudes about victims have begun to change. This is particularly true in cities, where crime is a growing problem.

Victimology, the study of the role of the victim, was introduced toward the end of the 1940s. Victimologists study the role of the victim from different points of view in an effort to learn more about why people become victims. The goal of victimologists is to change the attitudes of society toward victims through crime-prevention, education, and counseling. Victimologists aim to reduce the number of people who are victimized and to increase compensation for victims.

A new look at what is happening to crime victims is of utmost importance to everyone. First, consider who the victims of crime really are.

IMMEDIATE VICTIMS

Crime in Urban Areas

In some cities, even though the population has been declining in recent years, the total number of serious crimes has increased. According to Bureau of Justice statistics, one out of every three metropolitan households is likely to be touched by crime during the year. In small towns and rural areas the ratio is one out of four.

In 1980 *The New York Times* reported that residents of Los Angeles had been killing each other at a rate of more than six a day. Sometimes there were so many bodies in the morgue that people who processed them ran two days behind schedule. The number of murders had grown at the rate of 20 percent a year, with some murderers killing more than one victim.

Many people fear that crime is rising out of control to such a degree that they are almost certain to become victims sooner or later. The odds are that at least one person in eighteen will be a victim of serious crime in the coming year. The new organization known as National Victims of Crime reports that crime hit one out of every five families in 1981. One cancer specialist suggests that you have more chance of being murdered next year than of dying from cancer.

Random and Irrational Crime

In traditional "crimes of passion," the victim was usually a member of the murderer's family or someone intimate with the murderer. But today many victims are complete strangers to their attackers. This changing relationship between murderers and victims is of concern to many social scientists.

Marvin Wolfgang, a well-known professor of sociology and law at the University of Pennsylvania, notes that violent crimes are becoming more vicious and the chances of being hurt or killed in a robbery are increasing.

Almost everyone who follows the news agrees that violent crimes are becoming more random, more brutal, and more irrational. There is an apparent increase in killing for the pleasure of it. Again and again, one reads accounts of people who have been shot after giving up their money and jewelry at the demand of a thief. A typical example was reported in *The New York Times:* Three friends were out for an evening stroll when a young man pointed a gun at them. All three friends gave up their money without resistance. As they started to walk away, and for no apparent reason, he shot one of them to death.

The Wrong Place
at the Wrong Time

Along with the increase of random, vicious crime comes an increase of victims who find themselves in jeopardy without warning. Typical is the case of thirteen-year-old John Pius. He happened to ride his bicycle near the area where two teenage brothers were stealing a motorless minibike. The brothers thought John had seen them and might tell what they had done, so they chased him. John tried to escape them by pedaling around the schoolyard as fast as he could, but the fifteen- and sixteen-year-old brothers caught him, beat him, and stuffed pebbles into his mouth until he suffocated. Then they threw his body into a ravine behind the school. Although the crime John witnessed was relatively minor, the fact that he happened on the scene cost him his life.

Victims of Victims

Fear and suspicion often cause irrational and panicky reactions. For example, a sixty-six-year-old Bronx woman shot her husband to death in the belief that he was a burglar. There had been two break-ins in the course of one year in the Mangino apartment, prompting Mr. Mangino to buy a gun. He instructed his wife to shoot first and ask questions afterward. She followed that advice one afternoon when he left the apartment briefly to throw some refuse into the building's incinerator.

Mr. Mangino reentered the darkened hallway while his wife was napping on the living room sofa. Thinking that her husband was asleep in the bedroom, Mrs. Mangino reached for the pistol that she kept nearby for protection and killed her husband with a shot in the chest. Her fear of being victimized caused her to panic when she was startled from sleep.

This case is just one of many in which relatives have shot each other mistakenly.

Most Victims Are Young

Professor LaMar Empey of the University of Southern California recently conducted a crime survey showing that the likelihood of becoming a victim decreases with age. The most likely victims of crimes of violence and theft are young people between the ages of sixteen and nineteen. The next most likely age group includes those from twelve to fifteen years old. Professor Empey, whose study was based on federal crime statistics, found that young males are more likely to be robbed, assaulted, or murdered than young females.

In New York City, the Police Department reported that the person most often arrested for homicide is a male between the ages of sixteen and twenty. The most likely homicide victim is a male between the ages of twenty-one and twenty-five.

Overall, violence is most commonly committed by young males against young males.

The Role of Life-style

A victim's personality or style of life may contribute to his or her chances of being a victim. Prostitutes, homosexuals, and those engaging in promiscuous extramarital sexual adventures, heavy drinkers and gamblers, and those who display' large amounts of money or gems are more likely to be victimized by criminals than people who do not fall into these groups.*

How Real Is the Problem?

Not everyone agrees that your chances of becoming a victim are greater today than they would have been if you had lived long ago. Scholars who study the history of crime rates note that the homicide rate in Great Britain has been decreasing. Social scientists report that the trend in violent crime in Western societies in the last hundred years or so is downward. Those who study crime in terms of cycles over many years predict that the trend will be downward during the coming decade.

These facts may make one feel that things could be

---

*McNamara, Donald, and John H. Sullivan, "Making the Victim Whole," *The Urban Review*, vol. 6, no. 3, p. 21.

worse, but for those who live in high-crime areas where almost everyone knows a person who has been criminally victimized, the generalization holds little comfort.

There is no accurate count of the number of victims of crime. Crime surveys are inaccurate since many crimes remain unreported. In an effort to get a reliable estimate of the number of crime victims, the Bureau of Justice Statistics conducts National Crime Surveys. The Bureau includes crimes reported to interviewers by people over the age of twelve in a representative sample of about sixty thousand households. Their findings are reported in the *Bureau of Justice Statistics Bulletins*, which are available from the Bureau at Washington, D.C. 20531. Even these incomplete reports show that the rate of crime in the United States is alarmingly high.

According to the Bureau's statistics, people in the United States are murdered at a rate of one every twenty-four minutes; a woman is raped every seven minutes; a burglar invades a house every ten seconds; there is a serious crime every three seconds; and a car is stolen every twenty-nine seconds. According to some estimates there is one chance in four that your home will be burglarized during the next year. According to another estimate, that chance is one in three.

About one in every five persons who was victimized by a violent crime during one recent six-month interval was attacked more than once. If each crime had been inflicted on a different person, the number of victims measured by the National Crime Survey would more than equal the populations of New York, New Jersey, and Pennsylvania.

Whether the crime rate is slightly higher or slightly lower than it has been in past decades and no matter how the rate will change in the distant future, a frightening number of people today are becoming victims of murder, assault, rape, and other violent crimes. In almost all cases, attention is focused on the offender, while the victim is largely ignored.

However there is a growing recognition of the plight of the victim. This may be partly due to the greater number of victims who speak out. And it is partly due to the fact that crime, no longer contained in inner cities, is spreading to the suburbs and rural areas and touching a new group of citizens. As crime spreads, the way people have traditionally viewed victims tends to change. Those who have not yet been robbed, burglarized, or attacked suddenly realize that they too may soon be victims.

A third reason for this changing attitude is the growing perception that every crime affects many people besides the immediate victim. Awareness of the great number of these "hidden victims" also contributes to changing public attitudes.

HIDDEN VICTIMS

Even a minor crime has its hidden victims. Consider the following nonviolent crime. A young woman was sunbathing early in the season when few people had come to the beach. She dozed off with her wallet in the beach bag next to her. While she was asleep, a man strolled by, stopped, and quietly removed the wallet from the bag. When the victim awoke and gathered her things for her return home, she discovered that her wallet was missing.

After reporting the theft to the police by phoning from a nearby house, the young woman walked home. As she was nearing her house, she remembered that her house key was tucked inside her wallet. Suddenly, she became more angry and frightened than she had been, for she realized that whoever had taken her wallet had her address and the key to her house. She would have to have the locks changed as quickly as possible.

There were other, hidden, victims of this crime. There were the neighbors who had to help the victim break into her house, the victim's parents who shared her fears, her friends who are now afraid to fall asleep on the beach, and the students she had been tutoring who missed their lessons because the victim could not make her afternoon appointments.

Although this crime seems trivial compared to murder, rape, or other violent crimes, it illustrates that the number of victims in any crime may be unexpectedly large. The effect of any crime is not limited to its immediate victims. Many people share the pain, the hardship, and the fears that are the result of a crime.

In the case of John Pius, described earlier in this chapter, the pain and outrage of his parents was prolonged. It was not until two years later that a jury of eleven men and one woman reached a guilty verdict against the murderers. Even though the verdict gave the victim's parents some satisfaction, they will continue to be victims of the sad death of their only child.

Victims of Fear

The fear of becoming a victim plays a major role in the life-styles of many people who live in large cities. This is especially true among the elderly. One of the greatest anxieties is the fear of being mugged. Even though the data gathered by the National Crime Survey shows that the rates of crime against the elderly are comparatively low, as many as 23 percent of the elderly recently surveyed responded that they were more afraid of crime and vandalism than of changes in their own health. These fears may weigh far more heavily on the elderly than on any other age group.

Fear of crime is woven into the fabric of many city lives. Consider the Brooklyn executive who wears a bulletproof vest, has a pistol strapped to his shin, and keeps a guard dog that sits in front of his desk. Even in the most fashionable sections of many big cities, heavy metal bars "decorate" the windows of many buildings. The high crime rate and the likelihood of being victimized are popular topics of conversation in many large cities.

The fear of victimization can also affect an entire community, large or small. To some degree, all of the people of Atlanta, Georgia, were victims of the tragedies there in 1980 and 1981, when twenty-eight children were murdered. Anyone growing up in Atlanta during those years was at least touched by the fear of becoming a victim. Behavioral scientists agree that these gruesome murders have left psychological scars on many children that will last for years. And these children will in turn indirectly victimize people with whom they come in contact.

WE ARE ALL
VICTIMS OF CRIME

It is easy to see that, in the broad sense, everyone is a victim of crime. In addition to the billions of dollars that are spent in operating the criminal justice system, the cost of goods and services to everyone is inflated by shoplifting and white-collar crime. Vandalism decreases the quality of education, and increases the cost of operating and building schools and running public transportation. You are the victim of these crimes and many others.

2

FROM BLOOD FEUDS
TO THE
JUSTICE OF TODAY

EARLY JUSTICE

A caveman sits in front of his fire peacefully watching the sunset. Another man jumps out of the forest and attacks him. The victim fights back, killing the attacker. Now the attacker is the victim.

Before the development of more-sophisticated social groups, primitive people dealt directly with each other in a struggle for survival. When one man attacked another, the victim sought revenge under his own personal laws. The victim was also the "prosecutor" and the "judge," dealing out the punishment he deemed best. The criminal then became the victim of the person he had injured. There was a one-to-one criminal-victim relationship.

When primitive groups became more organized, the family took the responsibility for punishing offenders. When someone in the group became a victim, the whole group considered itself wronged. Suppose a man from one family attacked a man from another. The victim's family would take revenge on the offender's family. Since those involved were related by blood, the feud was called a blood feud.

Many people think a blood feud gets its name from the fact that blood was shed, but the term actually describes a feud based on blood relationships. L. T. Hobhouse in *Morals in Evolution* suggests the following problem created by the blood feud: One member of the Bear totem is killed by a Hawk. Now one of the Hawks must be killed by one of the Bears, but this may not be the end of the feud. The Hawks may stand behind *their* murdered clansman, killing a Bear in revenge. This continues from generation to generation in an endless vendetta.

Consider the idea that a kind of blood revenge continues to exist even in current times. Stephen Schafer, author of *Victimology: The Criminal and His Victim*, suggests that modern wars in which nations fight nations in an effort to weaken or destroy each other is an example. Here, as in primitive times, the victim and offender may be interchangeable.

THE LAWS OF SOCIAL GROUPS

In the history of the primitive group, it was often the victim who decided whether or not he or she had been wronged; there were no specific group laws that determined whether or not a person had become a victim. But the group had some idea of restitution in addition to retaliation in kind: the offender was punished according to the prevailing sentiments of the clan or tribe. Although there was no impartial third party, some rules did evolve. Certain forms of both compensation and retaliation with varying degrees of severity were recognized as proper within a group as well as between groups. For example, if a married man raped a married woman, the woman's kin group and her husband's kin group were affected and entitled to compensation. In addition to paying damages to these two groups, the rapist also had to pay compensation to his own wife's kin.

Retaliation and Compensation

Retaliation, the principle of using punishment to bring a quarrel to an end rather than allowing a blood feud to continue, was introduced at a fairly early stage in the growth of the social order. The simplest and earliest rule of retaliation is expressed in the Bible in the Book of Exodus in the famous passage "an eye for an eye and a tooth for a tooth." This view of punishment was formulated long before the time of Moses.

The well-known Code of the king Hammurabi, which was formulated about 1750 B.C., illustrates both retaliation and compensation (payment to the victim). It bases the type and degree of either on the rank of the victim.

The following penalties for assault and homicide in the Hammurabi Code give some idea of the relationship between offenders and victims at that time:

If a poor man has struck the strength of a plebian, he shall pay ten shekels of silver.

If a patrician's servant has struck the strength of a free man, one shall cut off his ear.

If a man has struck a man in a quarrel, and has caused him a wound, that man shall swear, 'I do not strike him knowing,' and shall answer for the doctor.

> If the doctor has treated a patrician and has caused that patrician to die, or has opened an abscess of the eye for a patrician with the bronze lancet and has caused the loss of the patrician's eye, one shall cut off his hands.

Although it has been suggested that some of the other provisions in the Code were designed to encourage commerce and trade rather than assist victims of injustice, it is interesting to note that there is some mention of the state's responsibility to the victim in the code. For example, the city or mayor is ordered to pay one *mina* of silver to the kinfolk of a murdered person.

As society became more socialized, many victims were awarded some form of compensation or restitution. As a matter of survival, or because of the influence of peace-loving individuals in tribes, peace was brought about through the use of compensation by the offender in the form of cattle or some other material payment. This calmed the desire for physical vengeance.

Composition

"Composition" was an early procedure used by barbarian tribes such as the Goths and the Franks. Composition might combine compensation for the victim with punishment or some form of revenge, for it developed in a variety of ways in different groups. In any case, it was a more practical way of avenging the victim than the blood feud.

In some ancient German tribes, even murder might be atoned for by a fine of cattle and sheep, thus averting quarrels that would be dangerous for the community. In other tribes, certain crimes were considered too grave to be expunged in any way other than by the spilling of blood. If the crime was less serious than murder or rape, it was usually punishable by fine. This custom lasted into the Middle Ages, a period of time when part of the fine went to the king. If the fine was not paid, the blood feud held.

THE CHANGING ROLE
OF THE VICTIM

So it can be seen that the role of the victim was changing. The earliest concept of punishment evolved from the need to appease the gods, who had not been respected properly. Later, it was felt that the wounds of the victim cried out for revenge. They were appeased by the blood feud or by retaliation against the offender. Compensation was an attempt to meet the emotional needs of the victim and atone for physical damage with the payment of money or services.

As the social sense of justice developed, so did the idea that a clan or tribe could suffer injustice. From this it was an easy transition to the idea that an even larger community could be the victim of injustice. As time passed, it was common for the king or head of the state to summon before him families involved in a blood feud and require them to keep peace. The community might claim a share of the victim's compensation, and as the government grew in authority, its share increased. A part of the composition went to the victim, while the other part went to the king or the community. In Anglo-Saxon England, compensation was called the *Bot*, and it existed along with the *Wite*, which was paid to the king or overlord.

A person who did not pay the fine or penalty ordered by the head of the community could be outlawed and thus denied the protection of the group. Such a person was in danger from outside enemies and from anyone in his community, since one was permitted to kill an outlaw with impunity. This threat of being outlawed helped to establish the authority of the court of early law.

As governments grew stronger, the victim's right to restitution grew less, and eventually the fine to the state replaced the compensation to the victim. The rights of the victim became separated from criminal law and became part of civil law. Harm done to the victim was no longer the central issue of a criminal case even though it had caused the case.

With the development of families, clans, tribes, and nation-states, the victim-offender relationship became less and less personal. When crime became a public affair, the victim became a less important figure in the proceedings. After the era of composition in the Middle Ages, "crimes" were generally considered to be offenses against the state, while an offense against an individual's rights became known merely as a "tort." Overall, the victim's position had deteriorated.

Special concern for the rights of the victim has begun to revive. Many groups have outlined plans to reestablish victim compensation, and some have made headway in this direction. At many conferences, it has been pointed out that modern laws are particularly weak in their consideration of victims; in the U.S. and Western European nations they appear to be harder on the victim than on the offender.

Family Violence

For centuries, a man was free to control his family in whatever way he wished. Wife beating, child abuse, and parent abuse were considered a private family matter, not a criminal offense; the authority of a man to discipline the members of his household was unquestioned. The United

States, which based much of its law on English Common Law, treated husband and wife as one person (the husband).

In the United States in the early nineteenth century, a man was permitted to chastise his wife or other family members physically without fear of being charged with assault and battery, but by 1870, wife beating was illegal in most states. This seems like an advance in the protection of women but it did not change matters very much. Few men who beat their wives were ever brought to court since criminal justice officials generally avoided interfering with family problems.

Spouse beaters, and adults who abuse children and the elderly, are coming under closer scrutiny at the present time, but there are still large numbers of victims who receive little or no protection from society at large. Child-protection agencies have made some strides since 1874. In those days, there were laws to remove animals from places where they were ill treated, but human victims had no protection. That year, a severely abused nine-year-old girl was taken to court on a stretcher because she was too weak to walk. Her case was instrumental in bringing attention to the plight of abused children. Since then, some progress has been made in helping to protect the infants, children, wives, husbands, and the elderly who become victims of domestic violence. However, much remains to be done. Courts are still slow to intervene in "family affairs."

No matter what the crime, there are many unprotected victims in the world of today. The justice system has changed greatly from the days when a victim had to depend entirely on the family, clan, or tribe, but victims today usually play an unimportant role in the courts of most countries. It is relatively rare for the victim to be fully compensated or "made whole" again.

3

THE CRIMINAL
AND
THE VICTIM

BLAMING THE VICTIM

A young man was mugged on his way home from work as he rode his bike through an urban park. Although he had taken this path many times, no one had ever questioned his riding there until after the mugging. Then his friends, his family, and his neighbors all asked, "Why were you there? Why did you go through the park alone? Why did you carry so much money with you?" The young man had the feeling that people were blaming him for being victimized.

So many people tend to blame the victim that an old joke about it still makes its point. Zero Mostel, a famous actor, used to do a sketch in which he represented a well-known Southern senator conducting an investigation of the beginning of World War II. He shouted with a mixture of triumph and suspicion, "What was Pearl Harbor doing in the Pacific anyway?" But blaming victims of poverty for living in areas where there is a high crime rate is not so funny. William Ryan's book *Blaming the Victim* is listed in "Suggestions for Further Reading," near the end of this book.

Blaming the crime victim is commonplace. Psychiatrists explain this seemingly unreasonable feeling by citing our universal need to find a rational explanation for violence. If people can believe that the victim deserved what happened, then they are reassured that such attacks do not occur at random. They feel in control, less subject to the threat of becoming victims themselves. This attitude quickly changes in a person who is victimized. But until then, the victim of a crime may be forgotten.

Albert Ellis, a noted psychologist, explains that people often need to find a particular reason for what has happened. Perhaps a mugging victim makes a slight move that the mugger interprets as dangerous. If the victim comes to harm as a result, people are quick to say that he brought it on himself by frightening the mugger. This satisfies the universal need to find some explanation for what has happened, farfetched though the explanation may be.

Here are some very brief accounts of murders that actually happened. How do you feel about the role of the victim in each case?

Seventeen-year-old Gregory became involved in an argument with some men over a game at an arcade. He was stabbed in the chest, the back, and the side.

Steve asked three strangers to help him start his car when the battery died. The strangers demanded ten dollars for their help. When Steve offered them five, they shot him.

Mr. Burgess lived in a high-crime neighborhood. He knocked on the door of an acquaintance, who greeted him with shots that killed him. The acquaintance claimed self-defense even though Mr. Burgess was not carrying a weapon.

A young woman was shot by a man who was gunning for her friend.

In each case it is possible to imagine some reason for the murder. For example, in the first two cases, the victims got into arguments with strangers. Mr. Burgess should have known that people living in the area were nervous and afraid. He might have prevented his own death if he had called to identify himself before knocking. One might say the young woman who was shot kept the wrong kind of company.

Finding reasons for blaming an innocent victim is all too easy. Sometimes, however, victims are indeed to blame, or partially to blame, for what has happened.

VICTIMS WHO PRECIPITATE CRIME

Studies of female murderers show that 40 percent had previously been abused by their victims. For example, Roxanne Gay of Clementon, New Jersey, a twenty-five-year-old student nurse, had repeatedly sought help from the police after being beaten by her husband who was a professional football player. The police merely told her husband to take a walk and cool off when he grew angry. Roxanne Gay knifed and killed her husband after another, allegedly brutal beating.

Another example of a battered wife clearly illustrates how the victim can precipitate the crime. After a long history of being beaten, Francine Hughes poured gasoline around her sleeping husband and ignited it. Francine and her husband were divorced, but she had returned to help nurse him back to health after a nearly fatal automobile accident. His assaultive behavior had characterized their marriage before the divorce. Now he continued to assault Francine, in spite of his injuries. On the day of the murder, he had beaten her several times. At the trial, the defendant claimed that she was driven to the murder by long years of physical abuse.

Both women were acquitted on the grounds of temporary insanity. In numbers of cases, juries have concluded that husbands killed by battered wives had precipitated their own fate to a significant degree. The degree to which the victim brought on the crime is a major factor in the outcome of these trials.

VICTIM PARTICIPATION

Can some victims avoid their fate? Many experts feel that some murders could have been prevented if the victim had acted differently:

A man and his wife were sitting in their car in the driveway waiting for a friend to join them. They happened to be near the ice cream store that four young men had planned to rob. The store was closed, so the young men cruised around in their car looking for possible targets. They noticed the man and his wife in the parked car, and three of the young men went to investigate, leaving the fourth behind. Hardly any time had passed when he heard a shot, and his friends ran back screaming to him to get out of there. As they sped away, one of the boys asked another, "Why did you shoot him?" The answer was: "Don't worry, I had to."

The victim, it seems, had reached for his wallet, trying to retrieve it from the robbers because he needed his credit cards for a trip that was to begin the following day. His reaction was understandable. However, the murderer did not care about the victim's reason. He was provoked by the man's resistance. The victim contributed to his own death by aggravating a person with a weapon who cared no more about taking a human life than he did about swatting a fly.

Obviously, the risk of being murdered increases when people place themselves in dangerous situations. For example, a hitchhiker takes a greater risk than a person who gets a ride with a friend or takes public transportation. People who walk alone in deserted areas at night are more likely to become victims than those who avoid such situations. Anyone who gets into a quarrel with someone who is agitated or upset is more likely to be a victim than one who refrains. Resisting an armed robber can increase the chance of being murdered. Nancy H. Allen has investigated murderers and their victims and presented the results of her study in *Homicide: Perspectives on Prevention.* She shows that some victims contribute unintentionally to their own violent deaths and some may play an active role, especially in "crime of passion" or the wife-beating cases like those described above. In these cases, it may be only a matter of chance that one becomes the offender and the other the victim. In a study of sixty cases, thirty-three people were found to have played a part in their own deaths. Sometimes, too, a person unconsciously wants to destroy himself or herself. Such a person may get into dangerous situations "accidentally on purpose."

CATEGORIES OF VICTIMS

According to some studies of crime-victim relationships, certain groups of people are considered high on the list of potential victims. Hans von Hentig was one of the first people to call attention to the role of the victim in a criminal act. He categorized victims according to social, psychological, and biological factors. The young were first on his list because they are weak and inexperienced. He described females as vulnerable. They are often assaulted sexually and may be murdered afterward to prevent them from identifying the criminal. Wealthy women are apt to be victims. They are targeted for robbery and they are usually physically weaker than the men who attack them. Hentig's list also includes the old, the mentally retarded, immigrants, minorities, the depressed, lonely people, and others.

Many victimologists have tried to sort victims into classes in an effort to explore how vulnerable different people might be and what parts they might play in the interaction between victim and criminal. In the relatively new science of victimology, the criminal-victim relationship is considered important in the understanding and judging of a crime. In Stephen Schafer's Book *Victimology: The Criminal and His Victim,* the following types of victims are described.

1. *Unrelated victims.* Many victims are just unlucky; they happened to be in the wrong place at the wrong time and have no relationship to the offender who has committed a crime against them. The criminal should carry full moral responsibility.

2. *Provocative victims.* These victims have done something to arouse or incite the offender to commit a crime. In some cases, the use of alcohol or other drugs blinds a victim to possible danger, clouds his or her judgment, and leads to action that results in being victimized. In such cases, the responsibility for the crime should be heavily shared, according to Schafer.

3. *Precipitative victims.* These people tempt the offender by their behavior, such as walking alone in the dark, which may be an invitation to robbery. Women who wear revealing clothing, according to Schafer, may entice men to rape. He admits that a perfectly socialized person could not be tempted or enticed into breaking the law, but he feels that these victims cannot be considered entirely blameless.

4. *Biologically weak victims.* These are the young, the old, the female, the disabled, the mentally retarded, who are easy prey but have no direct relationship to the criminal. According to Schafer, even though such people cannot help the fact that they are vulnerable, being easy prey precipitates the crime. He suggests that responsibility should be shared by the criminal and society at large, which should provide necessary protection for such individuals.

5. *Socially weak victims.* Recent immigrants and others who are not full-fledged members of the community are often exploited by criminals. They are targets, and here again, Schafer says the responsibility should be shared by the criminal and the society that is prejudiced against these victims as a group.

6. *Self-victimizing victims.* Alcoholism, drug addiction, and gambling are examples of the so-called victimless crimes in which the criminal and the victim are one. Schafer suggests that the responsibility rests on the victim-criminal alone and not on society. Not everyone agrees with this point of view since they see society as playing a major role in the environments of these people and see their problems as illness resulting partly from the environment.

7. *Political victims.* These are people who suffer violence at the hands of their political opponents. From a moral standpoint, says Schafer, they should be classed as having no sociological responsibility. Society may consider them criminals or heroes, depending on who holds the power.

This list is Schafer's attempt to examine systematically the criminal-victim relationship, which he considers the critical factor in understanding and judging crime.

New emphasis on the role of the victim and the increased interest in victimology indicate that many experts feel a need to consider the total picture before judging a criminal act. After taking into account the role and responsibility of the victim, if any, most victimologists claim that the offender should be made responsible for compensating the suffering of the victim.

While some groups focus their interest on the part the victim plays in the crime and others are mainly interested in helping the victim, almost everyone agrees that the status of victims has been neglected in the study of crime in society at large, and in the criminal justice system.

The late Supreme Court Justice Benjamin Cardozo is often quoted as follows: "Justice, though due to the accused, is due to the accuser also. The concept of fairness must not be strained till it is narrowed to a filament. We are to keep the balance true."*

---

*1934 Supreme Court decision, *Snyder* v. *Massachusetts*, 291 U.S. at 122.

4

UNDERSTANDING THE VICTIM

THE FEELINGS
OF VICTIMS

A mother whose son had been murdered returned to the murder scene again and again. She tried to imagine her son's feelings when he was mugged and his fears when he realized that the mugger had a handgun. Did he die immediately, as the coroner had assured her, or did he suffer for a long time? This mother still feels pain and loss although the crime was committed over seven years ago. She tells anyone who will listen about the "years of tears" that followed the tragedy. Once she thought that the United States was a place in which children could grow up safely if they stayed among "decent people" in "decent neighborhoods." She had always been certain that no one in her family would ever be murdered. Now she knows what it is to be a victim.

Bob Smith was the victim of a robbery. Bob had just stepped into the elevator in his apartment building when someone demanded his wallet. He gave it up without argument. After the thief left the elevator, Bob returned to his apartment and called the police. Then he showered for the second time that morning because he felt dirty. He was angry and he felt shamed. His friends told him that he was lucky to be unharmed, but Bob did not feel "unharmed." The emotional pain remained with him long after the actual day of the crime. Feelings of vulnerability and helplessness lingered for many weeks. Fear and caution became a part of his daily routine. He felt that he could no longer trust people.

HOW VICTIMS
REACT

People behave in different ways after they have been victimized. Some people find that one experience of being a crime victim is enough to make them move to a different neighborhood or to a location far away. This may be the case even if the crime was minor. Whether it involves the loss of a wallet or the loss of a child, the victim may want to get away from the physical location of the crime. Victims usually find, however, that their emotional scars travel with them.

Some victims simply give up. They adopt a philosophy of learning to live with the crime. They accept the inevitable feeling of being violated each time they are victimized. One man who was robbed twelve times insists that he has learned to live with being mugged. He says that when it is over, you just go on. He asks, "What else can you do?"

Other victims take action. After people become victims, they usually take a great interest in trying to make others appreciate how it feels to be victimized. They want everyone to understand what it is like. Although most victims believe that no one can really know how it feels to have someone invade your person or property, they want people to share their fears. They write editorials, letters to the editor, magazine articles, and books. Many suggest measures to reduce crime, such as stricter gun control laws, longer and tougher sentences for criminals, capital punishment for murderers, a stronger and better-equipped police force, and faster responses to emergency calls. Some victims stress prevention—the importance of getting at the roots of crime. Others form or join groups supportive of crime victims and their families. (Some of these activities are described later in this book.)

SPECIAL EMOTIONAL FACTORS

The quality and the severity of a victim's feelings depend on very subjective considerations. When property is taken, the victim's attachment to it plays a large part in the way the victim feels about the burglary. Maggie's home had been burglarized twice. In the second burglary, the last of her valuable possessions was taken. But when she told friends about the theft, she could talk of nothing but the loss of a small purse of no intrinsic value. The purse had belonged to her mother, and Maggie had childhood memories of carrying it when she played dress-up in her mother's clothes.

Sometimes the hostility of the criminal is more difficult for a victim to deal with than the loss of property. For example, when thieves burglarized the Russells, they also vandalized the house. They dumped everything from the drawers and took the sheets from the linen closet. But what upset Janet Russell most was the fact that they had walked all over the clean linen. She felt that this unnecessary and excessive destruction was evidence of a malicious intent.

The theft of an automobile causes special emotional problems for some victims. Just as their homes are extensions of themselves, so are their cars, and for some, the automobile is even more important than the home.

The threat of physical harm may leave a victim with lasting emotional wounds. Bill was walking down the street when a large man came from behind him and grabbed him just above the elbows in a technique muggers call "yoking." This technique prevents the victim from using a weapon even if he has one. The mugger threw Bill to the ground, pinned one arm under his knee, and placed the other knee in the small of Bill's back. He took Bill's watch and his wallet and ran off in a matter of seconds.

Bill lay on the pavement, dazed and helpless. He felt humiliated because he had not been able to protect himself. If Bill had known that police officials advise against trying to counter such an attack, he might have felt better. Police experts warn that unless the element of surprise is on their side, even people experienced in judo and karate may not be able to disarm a mugger. One martial-arts instructor believes that he would not try to defend himself if someone pointed a gun at him. He points out that a bullet can travel faster than his foot.

The circumstances in any victim's life also play a part in the reactions that follow a crime. Bill was especially vulnerable at the time he was mugged. He had just lost his job and was feeling depressed. If he had been feeling secure about his personal life, he might have recovered from the mugging more rapidly.

GUILT

Many victims suffer from a disproportionate feeling of guilt. Consider the following arson case.

A man helps his family leave their burning home and starts back just as the fireman runs from the side door with a baby tucked under his coat. He sees the fireman and feels relieved that everyone is out of the house. He goes to the line of children who stand dazed in spite of the attention of neighbors who are trying to comfort them. The father hugs each one of the children as he moves down the line. When he reaches the fireman who rescued the baby, the father calls another name. "Bobby?" he asks. "Where is Bobby?"

But Bobby was in the house. His body was found after the debris had cooled. Bobby was not the only victim of the arsonist who set the blaze that killed this boy. His father felt very guilty because he had not searched under the bed where his son had been hiding in fright. He felt guilty because he was alive and his son was not. All the brothers and sisters blamed themselves for not rescuing Bobby. Even the mother, who was in the hospital at the time of the fire, felt guilty because she had elected to go to the hospital at that time for an operation that could have been postponed. The whole family's guilt feelings are out of proportion.

The feeling of guilt might be partially assuaged if the victim could be the one to bring the offender to justice. In the case described above, the father looked forward to his day in court. But the emphasis throughout the trial was that the arsonist had broken a law against the state. Although he was a victim, the father played only a small part in the scene. He was merely a witness, not the plaintiff. The father felt that he had little role in bringing the offender to justice, and feelings of guilt and helplessness continued to plague him.

RAPE

Rape is one of the most traumatic and shocking of human experiences. Many victims of rape are especially conscious of being neglected, or even exploited, by the criminal justice system that is supposed to protect them and their rights. Many women avoid reporting the crime because of their feelings of shame, anger, and guilt, as well as fear of the treatment they may suffer during the trial. Although there has been some progress toward understanding the rape victim, much remains to be done before the feelings of these victims are widely acknowledged.

Bess Norton thought the man who knocked on her door was really the salesman he claimed to be. But soon after she let him in the apartment she realized that she had made a mistake; the man was a rapist. He held a knife at her throat and threatened to kill her and her child, who was sleeping peacefully in the next room. She kept telling herself that she was only having a nightmare. This could not really be happening.

After the rapist left, Bess went to check on her daughter, Jennie, to make certain that she had not been disturbed. Since Jennie was still sleeping peacefully, her mother decided not to waken the child. She was filled with conflicting emotions. Perhaps she should forget the whole thing. She felt too ashamed to call her parents, who had warned her about allowing strangers to enter the apartment. She hesitated to call the police for fear they would not believe her. At the same time, she was enraged against her assailant. She wanted him caught and punished.

Bess's primary feeling was of contamination and filth, and her immediate reaction was to shower before she did anything else. (Unfortunately, this feeling of wanting to wash away the experience makes many victims take action of this kind, but it destroys evidence.) Bess showered for a long time, then she scrubbed the whole bedroom. She continued to scrub anything that caught her eye until morning came. She was unable to take any rational action, unable to face any decision.

Finally, Bess called a friend, who came to stay with her, but nothing seemed to ease her feeling of isolation. In the days that followed, she wondered if she might be pregnant, if she might have contracted a venereal disease, and she wondered if her friend would tell others about her experience. Were people looking at her knowing that she had been the victim of rape?

Every time there was a knock at the door, Bess felt frightened and helpless. She wondered if the rapist might return, force his way into the apartment, and reenact the crime. Even though she realized that he could have forced his way inside, she continued to feel quilty about allowing the "salesman" to enter her apartment. She refused to tell her family, certain that they, too, would blame her.

Bess suffered typical reactions of a rape victim: for weeks she was extremely disorganized and had recurring fears of violence and death. She expressed a mixture of anger, fear, and anxiety through periods of crying, emotional upheaval, and restlessness. For many rape victims, there are long-range effects that outlast this critical phase. Such reactions as fear of crowds, fear of being alone, and fear of being followed are common. There is a long process of reorganization and coping.

Bess and many other victims of rape feel the effects for months, or even years, after the crime. Many suffer from a lost sense of security, diminished self-esteem, sexual anxiety, and a fear of the unexpected and strange.

For some women, the scars remain forever. Dr. Ann Burgess and her colleague Linda Lyle Homstrom, who have studied problems of rape victims extensively, write that an overwhelming majority of women are profoundly affected by being raped. In one of their studies, over 39 percent of the victims said that it took months to recover, 35 percent reported that it took years, and, as long as five years after the incident, 26 percent still did not feel that they had recovered.

DOMESTIC VIOLENCE

Violence in the family is a special kind of abuse from which the victims often suffer in silence. Some victims want to protect the spouse or parent who is the abuser, hoping that somehow the hurt will go away and the incident will never happen again. The abuser, who may be sincerely sorry, may persuade the victim that it won't happen again. But the abuse may be repeated over and over, sometimes until the victim must seek help from a doctor or an emergency clinic. Even then, victims often try to hide the reason for their injuries. Some are embarrassed. Often women and children are afraid that life at home will be even more difficult if the abuser is exposed. And they may have no other place to go.

Battered Wives

Even though life may be very unpleasant and the fear of injury or even death may be great, many battered women agonize over whether to leave home. Leaving may mean poverty, or it may mean leaving children for whom they feel responsible. Many women have a psychological dependence on men who mistreat them, for many of these men may be kind and generous most of the time.

It is easy to see why victims of family violence feel a special kind of pain. In addition to physical hurt there is the agony of knowing that someone you love, or someone you once loved, is treating you like an enemy who must be subjugated. A battered wife may feel that a husband treats her as his property. She feels helpless and isolated. She may have few friends because she is ashamed to let people know what is happening. This is true of many battered women.

Abused Children

Physically abused children, even when they are badly hurt, have been known to protect parents. They may fear further abuse if they do not hide the reason for their injuries, and they may also be ashamed to admit that a parent has been the abuser. Some children are abused by having to take on the role of parents instead of being taken care of by their parents. The children fill their parents' needs for love and comfort, but their roles as adults steal away their childhood.

Children often blame themselves for their parents' abuse, and this feeling may be reinforced by parents who are emotionally troubled. Most parents who abuse children have low opinions of themselves, and their children grow up feeling the same way.

Sexually abused children often suffer permanent psychological damage from fathers who rationalize that they are teaching the victim the facts of life or that the child has seduced them. Such fathers usually condition the children unconsciously when they are very young by sexually stimulating them under the guise of normal affection. As the little girls grow older, they associate this kind of behavior with fatherly love. By the time they are nine, most of these child victims become aware that sex with father is taboo. By then it is too late to change long-standing behavior patterns without the help of a therapist. For many, the abuse continues with an added burden of shame and guilt.

Dr. Alexander G. Zaphiris, an educator, social worker, and lawyer who has made studies of incestuous relationships and the feelings of victims, did a study involving female convicts. He found that 52 percent of the prostitutes in one penal institution had been victims of incest as children. Thirty-six percent of the felons and 25 percent of the women convicted of sexually molesting little girls were also incest victims.

No one knows all the feelings of children who are abused sexually, physically, and/or emotionally. It is known that an abused child may suffer from stunted physical, emotional, and intellectual growth.

Battered spouses and victims of child abuse are receiving more attention than in the past. But even today, thousands of cases of abuse go unreported and unnoticed. Most of the victims are neither rescued nor treated. Some estimates of the number of victims are unbelievably high. But many people in positions of authority are still hesitant to interfere in crime that takes place within families.

VULNERABILITY
OF VICTIMS

The feelings of victims are as varied as the victims themselves. Every crime is different, and, of course, every victim reacts differently even to the same type of crime. Often circumstances that have no connection with the crime play a part in a victim's ability to cope with his or her suffering. But many feelings are common to most victims, no matter what the crime. Anxiety, fear, or even terror is an almost universal reaction to being victimized. Many victims also feel shame, anger, helplessness, guilt, and confusion. They feel out of control.

A crime victim is usually more vulnerable and dependent than normal because confidence and self-esteem are lowered. He or she needs help from someone who cares about victims and knows how to help.

5

HOW TO HELP
A CRIME VICTIM

RESPONSES TO THE
FEELINGS OF VICTIMS

Saying the right things to crime victims can help to restore
their trust in themselves and others. Many people shy away
from those who have suffered the nightmare of serious
crime, but this is a time when victims need the support of
family and friends. Even the strongest individuals suffer
feelings of helplessness and anger until the crisis has passed,
no matter how minor the crime may appear to be to others.
When these people are suffering from feelings of self-hatred
and humiliation that may come after the incident, noncritical
expressions such as "I'm so sorry you had such a horrible
experience" and "It wasn't your fault" can be extremely
helpful.

Most people who want to help a crime victim just do
not know how. They tend to say all the wrong things.
Consider the following true story:

Mrs. Goodyear went to the neighborhood store one
pleasant afternoon just to buy milk. She knew she would not
be away from the house very long, so she did not bother to

close the kitchen window. Crimes were very rare where she lived, and it was common for neighbors to leave doors and windows open. When Mrs. Goodyear returned, she went toward the first-floor bedroom to get a sweater. As she entered the room, she saw the bathroom door closing. She thought perhaps her son had come home from school earlier than usual. Still, he would not ordinarily use the master bathroom and she had not noticed his book bag in the front hall where he usually left it. But who else could be there? She pushed on the door, but someone pushed back, closing the door and locking it. She called her son's name, but there was no response. Certain that her son must be playing a trick on her, Mrs. Goodyear was still not seriously alarmed. She walked around outside of the house to look through the window of the bathroom. As she approached the bathroom window, a man crashed through the glass of the storm sash and ran into the woods behind the house. Mrs. Goodyear hurried next-door and called the police. Not until the next day did she begin to shake with delayed reaction and shock. She told her friends about the experience and tried to describe her feelings. This is how they replied to her unconscious cry for help in a time of emotional stress:

One friend said, "It's lucky you came home when the burglar was in the house. He didn't have time to steal anything." Another friend suggested that Mrs. Goodyear go to a psychiatrist so she would not have nightmares about people entering her house. Here are some other remarks her friends made:

"How awful! But I would have called the police much sooner."

"Why did you walk around to see who it was? He might have killed you."

"The police won't help. Even if they find the man, the judge will let him off because he didn't take anything."

"Why did you leave the kitchen window open? I always lock all the windows before I go out."

"You're safe now. There is no reason to be so upset."

All of these people meant well, but they responded in ways that were either ineffective or hostile. Psychologists suggest that listening to a victim can be frightening to the listener because people are reminded of their own vulnerability. This fear makes them want to resolve the situation quickly, so they say something curt or terse to the victim.

Hostile listeners are people who react with anger when they are frightened. They may be judgmental, blaming the victim for the crime. Some people want the victim to be dependent on them and grateful for their help. Others feel that the incident illustrates injustice in the world at large, and they worry about themselves rather than thinking about the plight of the victim.

What can you say or do that will help a victim to cope with the experience and recover from it as quickly as possible?

WHAT TO SAY
TO VICTIMS

When the victim describes what has happened, it is helpful to restate his or her feelings with a remark such as, "You must feel terrified." You might ask what else happened, encouraging the victim to tell more and express feelings this way. Let him or her know that you realize it was a frightening experience. Show that you find it normal and justifiable for the effects to be long-lasting. If the victim complains that members of the family do not understand or that they are upset, too, express empathy. Say, "This must be hard for you." Don't try to explain the family's position.

Sometimes it is very supportive for the victim when you express your understanding of the guilt feelings that often result from giving in to an attacker without resistance. On the other hand, a person who has unwisely fought back may feel better because of having put up a fight. This is not the time to suggest that resisting might have triggered further harm.

If the person is a close friend, offer to spend some time at his or her home. Or invite your friend to spend some time at your home. In any case, do not give instructions to the victim. Empathy helps more than advice.

TRAINED VOLUNTEERS

Most crime victims are resilient and survive even if they are shaken by the experience. There are some cases where victims find that they have a new sense of pride because they survived the experience. They emerge from it with new strength. However, many victims are permanently scarred. Crimes leave them damaged physically and/or emotionally. Words that comfort are just the beginning of their need for help.

In some parts of the United States, there are victim services agencies that train volunteers to serve the needs of crime victims. There are close to a thousand programs that help in various ways, although there are not enough to help victims everywhere.

Victims of assault have special fears and physical problems that volunteers are trained to relieve. Many of these victims feel better about talking to someone outside their families, especially when they know that the listener has been trained to help.

Battered women, as mentioned earlier, have special problems in that many have no place to go and are not able to support themselves or their children. Helpers may encourage them to develop job skills, even while these women remain in the house with a husband who is violent at times. Many battered women need to be told that they are not alone in this kind of situation. They can be told about support groups and counseling that may be available to them.

In the case of sexual assault, there are many special concerns, including fear of pregnancy and venereal disease although the actual incidence of either is rarely the result of rape. Workers at a counseling center can see that victims receive proper medical attention as well as emotional support. Many victims of rape feel intense bitterness about the incident but need help in directing their anger where it belongs—against the offender. Some victims need to be reassured that they have a right to be very angry, even though this seems obvious to an outsider.

Child victims of sexual assault are very sensitive, and what is said to them can make a major difference in the amount of time it takes for them to recover. Children, like other victims, often blame themselves for the problem, and they need reassurance from an adult who has been trained in what to say to such a victim. Talking to a child who is a victim of incest is a task for professionals.

The family of a murder victim also has special problems. Many people have difficulty dealing with a situation in which a family member has died a natural death, and they find themselves especially uncomfortable with the family of a homicide victim. Those who are trained to work with such families report that many experience a crushing loneliness and have little hope that things will get better with time.

Charlotte Hullinger, whose daughter was murdered, reports that losing a son or daughter by murder is one of the most difficult experiences anyone ever has to face. She says that part of what makes it so hard is that few people know what to say and many find the subject too painful to talk or think about. She created an organization, Parents of Murdered Children, to help these victims know that it is possible to survive and even to experience meaning and joy in life after the grieving that is necessary for healing to take place.

Those who have experienced the tragedy of murder in a family receive strength and support from others who have been down the same road. Telling these victims about such self-help groups may be the best thing you can do for them.

If you are interested in working with victims, you can explore the opportunities in your community. Perhaps you will feel strongly enough to encourage the establishment of a victim service agency. A useful guide is the booklet *Building A Solution: A Practical Guide for Establishing Crime Victim Service Agencies* by Marjorie Susman and Carol Holt Vittert. It is available from the National Council of Jewish Women in St. Louis, Missouri.

Crime victim service agencies are places where the right things are usually said to help victims. Talking with a victim is just part of the help that they offer. There are also many other ways to help victims, as you will find in following chapters.

6

SERVICES
FOR VICTIMS

The voices calling for crime victim assistance have been growing louder during the past decade. Again and again, victims complain that the crime itself was only the beginning of their suffering. In response, the number of victim service agencies is increasing.

Mrs. Sloan's case sounds familiar to many elderly women. She lives in a large apartment building. Her income is limited, and she depends on the Social Security checks that arrive each month. One day she cashed her check and returned from the bank to find a tall boy standing at her doorway. He demanded her pocketbook and she gave it to him without resisting. Then he punched her in the face and body, fracturing several ribs before he fled with the pocketbook.

The teenage mugger was caught by the police, but released on probation. Mrs. Sloan felt the injustice bitterly. The criminal had gone free while she was left with financial and medical problems and with the constant fear that comes from being a victim of mugging. She felt that no one really cared about what had happened to her.

There were some services that would have given Mrs.

Sloan moral support and practical assistance had she known about them. (One of the problems in the victim assistance movement is making people aware that help is available.) Mrs. Sloan could have called a victim hotline where a member of the hotline staff would have provided her with emergency services such as counseling, help in obtaining money for rent, food, and other necessities, and help in replacing credit cards or other documents.

Many hotlines help people to apply for crime victims' compensation to pay medical expenses and restore needed income. If locks have been broken, they help to replace them. Where long-term help is needed, hotline workers make referrals to special agencies.

VICTIM SERVICE AGENCIES

One outstanding agency is the Victim Service Council, which was started by the St. Louis Section of the National Council of Jewish Women in November of 1977. This group was especially aware of the fact that many victims suffer twice, once from the crime, and again from the neglect of the community around them. The Council developed a wide range of services to help victims, from the teenager who has been knifed in a fight to the elderly woman whose purse has been snatched.

An organization in New York City, the Victim Service Agency, operates programs in all five boroughs throughout the city and has a bilingual staff to talk with victims who cannot speak English. Such agencies give victims both emotional and physical help.

Sometimes an agency sponsors a special program to improve services. An example is the Good Samaritan

Network created by Aid for Victims of Crime, Inc., in St. Louis, Missouri. In this program, a group of specially trained volunteers in each of the city's nine police districts was coordinated with the Police Department through a twenty-four-hour crisis telephone hotline. They created a unique neighbor-to-neighbor, community-financed coalition to aid crime victims in the city of St. Louis. The network's aim was to make immediate contact with victims of crime and to assist them from the moment the crime occurred throughout the ensuing weeks. Funding for the network was established through annual membership fees from individuals, churches, and business, civic, and community organizations.

Sometimes follow-up by a volunteer at a victim service agency is extensive. For example, the Victim Service Council of St. Louis reports the following case:

Young Terry V. was shot in the back and left for dead. Although the police pursued and prosecuted the criminal, the victim received no help other than initial treatment at a veteran's hospital. The shot left Terry paralyzed from the waist down. A volunteer from the Victim Service Council who found his case in the police files made a big difference in his future. Not only did she visit him in the hospital, but she arranged for a delay in his mortgage payments so that he did not lose his house. Her help included finding that the victim was eligible for some veteran's benefits.

When the volunteer worker visited Terry's home, she found that he was sleeping on a mattress on the floor because he could not afford the kind of bed needed by paraplegics. She called more than thirty agencies before she found one that would donate a bed that he could use. The volunteer also arranged for a mover to install the bed. This help was followed by job counseling. When the report on this case was written, Terry was still receiving help from the Council.

Many local victim service organizations are helped by national groups such as NOVA, the National Organization for Victim Assistance. The victim advocate program of NOVA is one of a number of programs that are trying to change the plight of the victim. NOVA represents society's increasing determination to eliminate the needless hardships that victims endure. Members are drawn from criminal justice and social service professions, from research and corporate organizations, and from the general public.

VICTIMS AS WITNESSES

Another kind of program is the Victim Witness Assistance Project of the American Bar Association's Criminal Justice Section. This group has prepared a manual to make state and local bar associations more aware of the problems of crime victims and witnesses and to help solve some of these problems.

Many people in the criminal justice system disregard special problems such as retrieval of stolen property that may be tied up indefinitely as evidence. Victims who are called as witnesses are often subject to insensitive interviewing by prosecutors, uncomfortable facilities at police stations or courthouses, unexplained summonses, or sudden changes in trial dates. These problems are magnified by the sense that law enforcement officials somehow blame the victim for the crime.

The American Bar Association, among others, is becoming more aware that victims, many of whom are also witnesses, find that their interests have low priority in the business of bringing a criminal to justice. Some victims feel that they are not just ignored by the system, but that they are used by it. The Bar Association is working to correct this situation.

The fact that many crimes go unreported is largely a result of the treatment victims receive in the criminal justice system. One man came upon a thief in the act of stealing his car radio. He chased the thief several blocks and caught him, with the help of a police officer. The thief was arrested and charged. That evening the man spent three hours in night court waiting to testify. However, because of a legal technicality, the prisoner was released without bail after a court appearance of sixty seconds. He was ordered to appear in court at a later date, at which time the victim appeared but the defendant did not. The victim was told merely that the failure of the thief to appear in court would be recorded and if he should ever be arrested again, it would be held against him. The victim deeply regretted having wasted his time.

In another case, a merchant who had been robbed found good reason to mistrust the criminal justice system. Long after the robbery, his window-display merchandise was tied up in court as evidence. The manager of his store spent a full day in court waiting in vain for the case to be tried. When the case did come to trial, the criminal, who had a record of fifty-one arrests, was released on bail, leaving him free to conduct "business as usual."

Since the participation of victims and witnesses is critical to the effective administration of justice, one can easily see the importance of reducing the problems of victims. Delays in court, postponements, and lack of communication about what is taking place compound the problems of the victim who has already suffered the crime.

KEEPING THE
VICTIM INFORMED

The National District Attorneys Association is among the victim's advocates. This group, along with others, is working toward the goal of a better system of notification for victims and witnesses. They suggest that victims be kept informed at every step about the progress of a case. In many courts this kind of system has already been put into effect.

Ideally, a confirmation letter is sent to tell the victim that a formal criminal charge has been filed against the defendant. This letter prepares the victim to receive the subpoena, the command to appear at the trial. (The subpoena itself is often delivered in person.) If the case is continued or postponed, a letter is sent to notify the victim and to specify the new trial date.

In many cases, a plea is settled before the trial date, eliminating the need for the victim-witness to appear in court. The Association advises that the victim should be notified and thanked for cooperating. If the offender was allowed to plead to a lesser charge, the letter should explain why this was accepted by the district attorney. If the defendant is found guilty, the victim should be notified.

Sometimes, the acquittal of the defendant seems like a personal affront to the victim. In this case, a letter of explanation from the district attorney can help by emphasizing the heavy burden of proof imposed in criminal cases as well as the importance of proving the case beyond a reasonable doubt.

Such a letter notification system keeps a crime victim informed of each major development as it occurs. One of its purposes is to eliminate unneccessary trips to court. Another system of notification that is helpful to victims is an around-the-clock alert system. A victim is asked to leave a phone number where he or she can be reached on the day that the appearance in court is scheduled. Throughout the day, the notification unit consults the prosecuting attorney or the judge to determine when a certain victim's presence will be required. The victim is notified in time to get to court. If the charge is disposed of by a guilty plea, if a previous case runs overtime, or if there is a continuance, the victim can be notified and saved from a frustrating trip to the court.

The cost of victim service agencies keeps them from being more prevalent and more extensive. However, most large cities consider expansion of such services crucial to the future quality of law enforcement in the United States. Some states, such as California and Connecticut, have been pioneers in showing how these services can be paid for without a burden on the taxpayers. Their courts assess a small fine, not exceeding twenty dollars, in addition to any other fines that are part of the defendant's sentence. These special fines help to fund victim-witness agencies and compensation.

VICTIM RIGHTS WEEK

Many volunteers who help to promote services for victims are recruited through special programs such as Victim Rights Week, sponsored by the National Organization for Victim Assistance (NOVA). Public support for the program has increased steadily. In 1980, about half of the states participated in this week. By 1981, the week of April 20–26 was officially designated as National Victim Rights Week, with ceremonies taking place in all fifty states.

According to NOVA, the main purposes of Victim Rights Week are:

To increase public awareness of the problems experienced by victims and witnesses;

To articulate the rights that should be accorded victims and witnesses;

To alert legislators and public policymakers to the need for programs for victims and victim assistance;

To increase public awareness of the availability of victim compensation programs where such programs exist, and to encourage their enactment elsewhere;

To help state and local programs band together to learn from one another and to win greater public support for their community services.

Most of the hundreds of victim-witness service projects throughout the country also share the following goals:

To enhance the quality of justice by satisfying the emotional and social needs of crime victims and witnesses;

To increase the willingness of victims and witnesses to cooperate with the police and prosecutors after they have reported a crime.

7

TOWARD JUSTICE
FOR VICTIMS

In recent years, there has been a growing tide of support for the idea of giving direct aid to victims. Direct aid commonly takes two forms: restitution and compensation. Many people use these terms interchangeably, but they represent two different things. Restitution usually means repayment by the offender to the victim who suffered financial loss as a result of the crime. Compensation refers to amends made to the victim by society rather than by the offender. It is paid by local or state governments.

RESTITUTION

Restitution payments may be made based on the value of the stolen or damaged property; medical expenses may be paid for the victim's crime-related injuries; or payments may cover wages lost as a result of absence from work. Payments may also be made for services obtained by deception.

Restitution may be used in a broader sense as well. Here are three examples of restitution:

Ralph's offense was breaking and entering a neighbor's house, where he stole silver flatware that he planned to sell for money to buy drugs. When Ralph was caught, he still had some of the silver in his possession. The value of the missing silver was determined, and the court ordered Ralph to pay for this through working for the neighbor. Part of his sentence was to care for the lawn on the neighbor's property for the entire summer. (Ralph would have preferred some other penalty; working for his former victim was very embarrassing. The victim felt that he was being generous in allowing Ralph to repay the loss in this way, and he had no intention of embarrassing Ralph.)

Jim was assigned a different type of restitution. He was convicted of stealing at a hardware store where he worked. Part of his salary was held back by the owner every week until the owner was fully compensated.

Mary's restitution took the form of community service, since the victim preferred not to have any contact with her. Her crime was vandalism, so she was ordered to repaint the walls of a day-care center. Sometimes this form of restitution is used when the victim wants no involvement with the offender.

Many people feel that restitution is not practical because offenders seldom have the means to make full restitution and the monitoring of any long-term arrangement is often difficult. However, many programs have shown worthwhile results. For example, the national program known as Restitution Initiative reports that less than 9 percent of young offenders committed new crimes while still in the program. Restitution Initiative is run by the Office of Juvenile Justice and Delinquency Prevention. Most of the referrals were young people who had been charged with burglary. Most of the restitution took the form of community service, but there were also several thousand hours of direct service to victims and more than $600,000 in cash payments to victims.

A program in Seattle, Washington, is cited as an example of how successful the idea of restitution can be. In one recent year, the number of commitments to juvenile detention centers decreased by 26 percent in areas where the program was used while they rose by 88 percent in other areas. Much of this change was attributed to the use of restitution.

This is how the Seattle program functions. Suppose a young man admits to vandalizing a school and appears before a panel of the Seattle Community Accountability Board. This panel consists of five or six members of the community, and it includes at least one young person. The panel, in collaboration with a representative of the Youth Services Board, decides upon an appropriate service or sum of money, or both, to be provided to the victim or to the community. The vandal might be told to pay the cost of repairing the damage and might also be asked to work in a hospital for a given period. The assignment is monitored by the representative of the Youth Services Board.

Most of the cases that come before the Seattle Community Accountability Board involve shoplifting. Other offenses include vandalism, first-time burglary, auto theft, and breaking and entering. Both the community and the offenders seem to be benefiting from this program.

While accurate figures are not available for the amount of restitution paid to victims throughout the United States, it is estimated to be millions of dollars. However, at present restitution reaches only a small percentage of victims.

COMPENSATION

There are several arguments for government compensation as opposed to restitution by the offender. After being fined by the court, offenders may be left without any assets, and imprisonment usually makes it impossible for them to earn money to compensate their victims. (It has been suggested that adequate pay for prison labor would make it possible for offenders to pay some restitution to victims. However, prisoners are not usually paid for their labor, so there has been no way to test this theory adequately.)

About two-thirds of the states in this country have compensation laws for certain classes of crime victims. Laws vary, but they are based on the rationale first that the state has a duty to protect its citizens from crime. If it fails to do so, the state thereby incurs an obligation to the victim. Second, the laws take into account the fact that most offenders are unable to make restitution themselves. Finally, there is a widely accepted principle that the state should aid all unfortunate victims of crime as a matter of general welfare policy. Most compensation plans are concerned primarily with assisting needy citizens in coping with a financial catastrophe due to crime.

To be awarded compensation, crime victims must also be shown to be totally innocent of provoking the crime. In some states, the victims must show that they suffer financial hardship, and all states require that compensation from insurance companies and other sources be deducted from awards.

Compensation helps to alleviate the feeling victims have that they are doubly victimized: once by the offender and once by the criminal justice system. The following sarcastic words of the Belgian representative at the Paris Prison Congress of 1895 are often quoted in connection with restitution and compensation:

> The guilty man lodged, fed, clothed, warmed, lighted, entertained, at the expense of the state in a model cell, issued from it with a sum of money lawfully earned, has paid his debt to society; he can set his victims at defiance; but the victim has his consolation; he can think that by taxes he pays to the Treasury, he has contributed toward the paternal care, which has guarded the prisoner during his stay in prison.*

Although the general concept of compensation dates back to the Code of Hammurabi, most modern compensation programs in the United States were set up after 1960. The New York State Crime Victims Compensation Board was established in 1966, and by 1980 compensation had been awarded to fourteen thousand victims and dependents of victims who died as a result of a crime. Typical of the latter are two widows who came before the New York Board recently.

One claimant is the widow of a thirty-eight-year-old man who was shot to death during a holdup. Another claimant is the widow of a sixty-five-year-old man who was found at the foot of a subway stairs lying in a pool of blood. He had six stab wounds in the chest, back, and neck. In both cases, the victims' widows received $1,500 for burial expenses, the maximum allowed by the statute and $8,805 for

*Summary Report, the Paris Prison Congress (London, 1895).

loss of support. In addition, they receive a monthly award of $285 which they will continue to get until the total reaches the statutory maximum of $20,000.

In one recent year, the New York Board awarded financial aid to 2,458 people. Eight hundred others continued to receive aid from previous years. Of course, not all who apply are eligible for compensation. About 40 percent of the formal applications result in awards. However, in New York and in many other states where compensation is available, there are many eligible people who do not know that they can receive compensation.

A BILL OF RIGHTS
FOR VICTIMS

One approach to making victims aware of their rights as victims can be the use of a card that has been called a counterpart to the "Miranda" warning (the notification to arrested persons that they have the right to remain silent and to have counsel present).

The National District Attorneys Association has suggested the following "bill of rights" for victims:

You have the right as a crime victim or witness:

To be free from intimidation;

To be told about compensation available to victims for their injuries;

To be told about social service agencies which can help you;

To be assisted by your criminal justice agency.

On March 21, 1980, the Wisconsin state legislature passed a bill of rights for victims and witnesses of crime that has been suggested as a model for other states by experts in this field. The Wisconsin Department of Justice is charged with the responsibility for the administration of the program, while its development and implementation are the responsibilities of individual counties.

According to the Wisconsin bill, victims and witnesses of crimes have the following rights:

To be informed by local law enforcement agencies and the district attorney about the final disposition of the case.

In certain cases, to be notified when the perpetrator is released from custody.

To be notified if court proceedings to which they have been subpoenaed will not go on as scheduled.

To receive protection from harm and threats of harm arising out of their cooperation with law enforcement and prosecution efforts, and to be provided with information as to the level of protection available.

To be informed of the financial assistance and other social services available to those who are witnesses to or victims of crime, including information on how to apply for the assistance and services.

To be informed of the procedure to be followed in order to apply for and receive any witness fee to which they are entitled.

To be provided, whenever possible, a secure waiting area during court proceedings that is not in close proximity to defendants and families and friends of defendants.

To have any stolen or other personal property promptly returned by law enforcement agencies when no longer needed as evidence.

To be provided with appropriate employer intercession services in order to minimize an employee's loss of pay or other benefits resulting from court appearances.

To see a speedy disposition of the case in order to minimize the stress on the victim or witness.

THIRD-PARTY LAWSUITS

In addition to the progress that has been made in the number and quality of victim-witness service agencies and in the areas of restitution and compensation, other kinds of efforts are helping victims. Rape crisis centers, and shelters for the victims of family violence have increased. The introduction of court monitors who watch proceedings helps to make certain that the victims' rights are protected at every stage from the initial charge through sentencing and the imposition of restitution or probation.

One area where there has been a dramatic increase in action is in the number of third-party suits. In a two-party suit the victim can sue the offender, but the offender seldom has the ability to pay any damages. However, the victim may also sue someone else whose negligence made the crime possible. This is known as a third-party suit. A famous case

in point is that of the singer Connie Francis, who sued the
Howard Johnson Company after being raped in one of their
motels. The two parties directly involved were Miss Francis
and the rapist. The third party, Howard Johnsons, was held
negligent for failing to provide secure locks on the doors of
the motel rooms. In this case, the singer was awarded one
and a half million dollars. Before the Connie Francis suit,
many lawyers assumed that courts would not grant damages
against third parties in such cases.

Frank Carrington, a long-time spokesman for the
victims of crime is executive director of the Crime Victims
Legal Advocacy Institute at Virginia Beach, Virginia. The
Institute is a nonprofit law firm that offers free consultation
to lawyers with victim cases such as third-party suits. Mr.
Carrington also serves as vice-chairman of the Victims
Committee of the American Bar Association's Section on
Criminal Justice. He says that he has been contacted at the
Institute by well over five hundred lawyers in the last few
years. In addition to providing advice for third-party suits,
this nonprofit group sponsors programs that involve public
education, and consultation with policy makers such as
judges and legislators. It also presents workshops, lectures,
and seminars on the legal rights of victims. Since its
founding in 1979, the Institute has received national publicity
and has provided help for attorneys and others from every
state in the union who are concerned with the rights of crime
victims.

The most difficult hurdle in suits against government
bodies has been the concept of "sovereign immunity." Mr.
Carrington says that in the broadest sense, this bars any
claims against the state. An example is the case filed by the
father of a murdered boy. The problem of immunity led to a
long and involved legal battle. Five-year-old Jonathan was
the victim of seventeen-year-old James F. Fisher, III, who

had a long record of sexual assaults on children. In spite of the fact that he told police a year before the murder that he would kill his next assault victim to prevent the child from informing on him, Fisher was given a weekend furlough from a juvenile detention center and released in the custody of his mother. The night after Fisher went home, he was seen dragging the body of Jonathan, whom he had assaulted sexually and then strangled. James Fisher was tried as an adult, convicted of murder, and sentenced to life imprisonment.

After the tragedy, the father of the murdered boy filed a million-dollar wrongful death suit against the county. He charged the county with gross negligence for releasing James Fisher and for not giving appropriate warning of his threat. After years of legal battle, he was denied on the basis of another case in which the Supreme Court of the United States ruled that state statutes giving immunity to parole boards do not violate the United States Constitution.

However, an increasing number of victims do appear to be succeeding in their third-party suits, and the Crime Victims Legal Advocacy Institute is providing support.

PUBLIC
EDUCATION

Another approach to helping victims is that of the Oregon-based National Association for Crime Victims' Rights. This association is a nonprofit corporation dedicated to "restoring the rights of America's innocent and defenseless victims of violent crime." This group hopes to accomplish its objective through action, education, and training within the nation's crime-conscious communities so that "crime is less attractive and profitable for those who commit or promote it."

WHO SHOULD
BE ELIGIBLE?

People who argue against compensation programs fear that some victims may be tempted to exaggerate their injuries in order to get more money and others may claim falsely that they were victims of armed robbery or some other crime, when in fact no crime has taken place. Even legitimate victims may be viewed as ineligible for compensation.

Some groups that promote the rights of victims suggest that the possible responsbility of the victim in the crime must be considered before awarding compensation. As we have seen, certain life-styles render people more susceptible to victimization than others. And what of cases where the victim obviously precipitates the crime? By what standard can we judge just what part a victim plays? Many such questions make the use of compensation or restitution complex. One suggestion for overcoming this problem is to use the criminal court to judge the role of the victim in the crime. However, this has many drawbacks, including the placing of the victim "on trial," the expense of counsel, and the burden on an already overloaded court system.

Other groups take the position that offenders should be held responsible for their actions no matter how much they are provoked. In some cases of sexual assault, defense attorneys have argued that the victim seduced the alleged rapist. Even young children have been accused of precipitating rape. However, those who feel that the offenders should be held accountable for their actions, believe that the victim should be compensated nonetheless. They point out that the offender could have refrained from committing the crime.

How one considers the rights of victims, then, varies widely depending on the nature of the crime, the relationship between the offender and the victim, and other factors that pertain to any individual case. However, with the increase in the crime rate, more people feel that the rights of victims must be considered as much as the rights of the accused.

The victims movement is sometimes considered to be a sign of revolt against the criminal justice system. Victims of crime are speaking out about the way the system has treated them. They are demanding more respect and compassion through a variety of programs.

8

REDUCING THE RISK OF BECOMING A VICTIM

How can you avoid becoming one of today's millions of crime victims? Certainly, no one is immune. Everyone is a potential victim. But some people are more likely to become victims than others.

How can you protect yourself in the streets and in your home? How helpful are locks and alarm systems? If you are attacked, should you fight back? Should you give the muggers what they want? There are no foolproof answers, but here are some suggestions that may help you to reduce your chances of becoming a crime victim.

First, consider how muggers select their victims. A study by Elizabeth Grayson of Hofstra University showed which people are most susceptible to violent crime. She videotaped pedestrians at random and showed these tapes to convicted assailants. The assailants were asked to select the people they would be most apt to mug. Since mugging is one of the kinds of crime to which older people are most vulnerable, it is not surprising to find that women over forty-five were rated as easy marks. But some characteristics other than age and sex applied. Uncoordinated people seem to be vulnerable. Most people walk heel to toe, but the muggers showed preference for people who pick up an entire foot each time they take a step. Potential victims swing each arm forward with the same leg rather than swinging the right arm as the left leg moves forward and vice versa. To muggers, these characteristics may reveal poor physical coordination.

You cannot do much about your age, sex, or coordination, but there are some common-sense precautions that you *can* take.

IN THE STREET

In the Grayson study, people who walked as if they had a purpose and seemed to know where they were going were not as popular with muggers as those who seemed less sure of themselves. It appears that a person who looks frightened is in greater danger than one who looks confident. If you walk briskly, you will probably avoid becoming a victim of street mugging.

The most important rule in reducing your chances of being mugged is to stay alert without appearing to be frightened. If you turn around now and then while you are walking, you may even attract a mugger, so you should be cautious without being obvious about it when you feel you are in a danger zone. After all, most people can listen to the radio while driving a car and still remain alert to traffic hazards. This awareness amounts to a sort of sixth sense. You can develop this kind of awareness when you are walking, too.

Where you walk on a city street can be important. Walking near buildings rather than in the middle of a sidewalk gives opportunity to muggers hiding in doorways or alleys. Sometimes it is safest to walk in the middle of the street.

Suppose someone seems to be following you. You hear the increased pace when you walk faster, and you feel uncomfortable. Test the follower by crossing the street and after a short while crossing back again. If the footsteps continue to follow, think about which way you can run and where you might get help. By being alert, you have eliminated the mugger's weapon of surprise.

Suppose you are certain that someone is following you but you cannot see a place to run or anyone to ask for help. If you see a lighted window, look up at it and shout to an imaginary friend as if someone were looking down at you. Forget about appearing foolish.

Lights and noise make good defenses. Even though each situation is different, screaming is usually appropriate. It lets people know that you are in trouble and even if no rescuer is present, it may frighten a would-be mugger who does not want to attract attention.

Screaming for help can sometimes prevent a crime, but calling "Fire!" is considered better than calling "Police!" Many people will avoid getting involved if police are called. It they think there is a fire, they come out of their apartments, if only to protect themselves.

How you carry your money can also reduce your risk of becoming a victim. A man who carries his wallet in his back pocket is more vulnerable than one who carries his wallet in a front pocket where pickpockets cannot remove it inconspicuously. A woman who holds her pocketbook near her body without obviously clutching it is safer than one who walks along with pocketbook in hand or dangling by a handle. Shoulder bags should be held near the body. A woman who clutches a pocketbook tightly or a man who keeps patting his wallet gives a clue to an experienced mugger who reasons that such a person may be carrying a large amount of money.

Many people are mugged as they fumble in pockets or handbags for transportation money or keys. If you often walk to a bus stop or subway in high-crime areas, have your fare readily available. Car keys should be available, too, so that you do not have to place packages on the car while fumbling for keys to unlock the door. The same is true of house or apartment keys.

Some safety experts suggest that you should carry a coin taped in a safe place to be used in a phone booth. Phone booths may be good places to escape muggers. You can lean against the door from the inside to prevent another person from entering while you call the police.

Sometimes muggers travel in automobiles, using a technique that begins with asking for directions. When a person in a car calls to a pedestrian for directions, it is natural for the pedestrian to walk over to the car. The driver or a passenger is in a position to open the door and pull the pedestrian into the car. This system has been used for robbing and kidnapping. Most people who ask for directions are perfectly innocent, but you can cooperate with them by calling from the curb.

Sometimes a mugger will invade a car that has stopped for a traffic light or stop sign. The mugger yanks open the door and gets in. It has been suggested that in such a case the driver can hit the horn, but doing so may provoke the intruder to violent action. If someone tries to enter your car, disregard the red light and drive away quickly while blowing the horn. (And of course, keep your doors locked in any dangerous area.)

MUGGERS
IN BUILDINGS

As many as half of all muggings take place inside buildings, especially in hallways, elevators, and laundry rooms. Muggers have their own techniques for elevators. John was the victim of such a scheme when he entered the elevator with another man. John had a feeling that the man looked suspicious, but he relaxed when the elevator stopped at the next floor and another man got on. Unfortunately, the two men were working together. John was attacked by one while the other removed his wallet.

If you feel that you are in a dangerous situation in an elevator, pushing a number of buttons may help. Stopping the elevator at many floors has been known to deter muggers.

If you come home and discover that a burglar is there, retreat to a neighbor's house or apartment and call for help from there. If someone comes to your door asking for help, perhaps because there is an accident in the neighborhood, don't open your door. Offer to call the police or an ambulance rather than allowing a stranger to enter.

SELF-DEFENSE:
GIVING IN OR
FIGHTING BACK?

Many victims must decide what to do when they come face to face with someone who threatens them personally. There is no easy answer, for each case is different. Very often, one can avoid becoming a victim by acting quickly and sensibly. For example, two girls were playing in the woods when a man tried to assault them sexually. One girl escaped and had to decide whether or not to go directly to the help of her friend or run to the nearest house for help. She made the intelligent decision and ran for help. As a result, her friend was rescued and both girls were safe.

People who give advice about self-defense do not always agree. In general, experts advise that a victim cooperate with an attacker unless there is danger of being murdered. Each situation calls for a personal evaluation and decision making at a time of great emotional stress. Some people feel compelled to resist, but there are many tragic examples of people who were beaten or killed because they did not readily give up their money.

In most cases, the odds are stacked against the victim, so it may be unwise to resist. Valuables can be replaced, but a life cannot. Even hesitation in submitting to an attacker may cause the thief to panic. So can a quick move. It is difficult for the victims to consider the emotional state of the muggers who are robbing them, but experts warn that most muggers are as frightened as their victims. Cooperating with a thief may help him or her to remain calm.

Victims, too, should also remain calm, according to those who have studied ways of protecting oneself. This sounds like advice that is impossible to follow. When one comes face to face with the threat of death, legs may buckle and the body may be numb in anticipation of pain. Or blind rage may cloud the victim's judgment. But a victim's reaction appears to set the tone of the crime. One woman angrily told a man who was stealing her personal property that she would never forget his face. He reacted by shooting and blinding her.

Escape is the victim's most important aim if survival is at stake. Some people try to protect themselves by kicking, but actions of this kind usually cause more violence by the attacker. Dramatic techniques are risky, although they may sometimes be effective.

Fred is an elderly man who was successful in using such a technique. He was grabbed from the back and a hand was slapped over his mouth. Fred's hands were still free; immediately, he grabbed the little finger of the attacker's hand and pulled down and away, hard. At the same time he drove the heel of his foot into the attacker's foot. He took the mugger by surprise, and the pain in the two sensitive places caused the mugger to loosen his grip. Fred escaped by running away and screaming for help. This was effective, but dangerous. Anyone who decides to use such a technique must do so quickly and forcefully. The element of surprise is crucial.

Jane had learned how to react quickly to a two-handed rear choke. One evening, a man grabbed her when she was walking home from the store. Immediately, she dropped her packages, kicked the attacker's shin, raised one arm above her head, and pivoted around to break his hold. She came down hard with her fist to the side of his neck as she stepped away. Then she ran, blowing the whistle that she kept in her pocket. Some experts recommend this technique, but others think it is dangerous for the victim, who usually is not as strong as the attacker and lacks the element of surprise.

Stamping down on an instep, and grinding with all your weight, striking the groin, scratching at eyes with a key, and using an umbrella as a bayonet may work, but these actions must be fast and expert or they may only result in further violence to the victim. Many experts recommend practicing such techniques harmlessly with a friend. In most cases, it is best not to resist unless you are well trained in the techniques of fighting back.

IDENTIFYING
THE ATTACKER

Victims should try to remember as much as possible about a mugger. It takes conscious effort to remember some of the things in the following list, but if you do, there is a much greater chance that the attacker will be apprehended. Try to remember:

> Height
> Weight
> Race and complexion
> Hair color
> Eye color
> Eyeglasses
> Whether eyes seem alert or droopy
> Approximate age
> Any visible scars, tattoos, or other marks
> Clothing colors and styles
> Direction of escape
> Any license numbers
> Description of vehicle
> Description of weapon

It is best to concentrate on physical features rather than clothing. If you make comparisons between the mugger and yourself, height, weight, and hair color are more easily estimated. Remember that clothing can be quickly changed after an incident.

PROTECTION AGAINST THEFT: LOCKING UP

Locked doors and windows obviously reduce the risk of becoming a crime victim. Many people leave their car keys in the ignition or under the seat or in a "secret" hiding place in the car. Most car thieves are knowledgeable about hiding places, no matter how "secret." The same is true of keys that are hidden outside the house. Leaving a key with a good neighbor is a better way to keep an extra key available.

Sondra always kept a key under the doormat. Just before she took her planned vacation, the key disappeared. She began to wonder if someone who knew she was going away had taken the key in order to burglarize her house while she was on vacation. She had all the door locks changed before she left, a project that was both expensive and inconvenient.

Many people say that a burglar will get into the house no matter how many locks are on the doors and windows. They think it is a waste of time to lock them. They do not realize that most burglars give up on places where entry takes more than a few minutes and enter another house or apartment where they can get inside easily. Breaking windows makes noise that might call unwelcome attention. The longer it takes a burglar to enter, the greater the chance of getting caught. Time is the burglar's enemy.

Although locked windows and doors deter most burglars, there are some who have special techniques for dealing with them. They dress well so that they will not be noticed in an expensive neighborhood, and they carry a set of tools the size of toothpicks which they use to spring the cylinders of door locks. This kind of burglar is known as a pocket operator because he or she usually steals only small things such as credit cards, jewelry, bankbooks, and cash. Sometimes, the homes that are robbed are so undisturbed that the owner does not realize what has happened until several days later.

Another type of burglar is known as the "smash and grab" thief. Such a thief uses a body-and-fender puller from an automotive store to extract the cylinder of the lock. A more expensive kind of tool that can be used for the same purpose and is quieter is a hammer that operates hydraulically. This kind of burglar typically carries away television sets, stereos, furs, oriental rugs, and other large, valuable items along with smaller items. And there are burglars who force open doors with jimmies, crowbars, large screwdrivers, or even just a heavy kick.

ALARM SYSTEMS

Many people reduce their chances of becoming victims by purchasing alarm systems. Pressure mats set off an alarm when a would-be intruder steps on the mat. They are usually hidden under rugs, stairways, or behind doorways. Systems that work by a photoelectric beam activate an alarm when the thief unknowingly crosses its path. Ultrasonic devices set off alarms when any kind of motion disturbs the sound-wave pattern.

Infrared alarm systems are popular because they are easy to install and less expensive than some other alarm systems. An infrared detector sounds an alarm when a person enters or leaves the area at which it is directed. This alarm reacts to abrupt changes in heat, but it is not activated by normal changes in air temperature, which take place more slowly than that caused by the intrusion of a person's body.

These are just some of the alarm systems that people are using to protect their property from thieves. Although many of these methods work very well, it sometimes seems that only the old system of moats and turreted castles is really foolproof.

The greatest disadvantage of using alarm systems is the accidental tripping of alarms, which causes much trouble for police. In some communities, owners whose alarms go off without cause frequently are fined. False alarms may discourage neighbors from responding to the system, too.

HELPING TO PREVENT CRIME

Helping to prevent crime also reduces the risk of becoming a victim. You can help in many ways, from supporting programs such as Big Brothers and Big Sisters to writing your legislatures to encourage them to support drug rehabilitation programs and other crime prevention measures. Volunteer tutors in schools contribute to the reduction of crime by helping young people learn to read and write; literacy helps people to get jobs, and jobs help people to stay free of crime.

The list of ways that people can help to reduce the risk of victimization appears endless. For information about local programs call your police department or any community agency that places emphasis on victim-witness assistance or crime prevention. Neighborhood Watch Programs are helping to reduce crime in many communities. National Organizations such as NOVA (National Organization for Victim Assistance), the National District Attorneys Association, and National Victims of Crime can provide information. Their addresses are given in the section beginning on page 97.

SUGGESTIONS FOR FURTHER READING

Allen, Nancy H. *Homicide: Perspectives on Prevention.* New York: Human Sciences Press, 1980.

Bard, Morton, and Dawn Sangry. *The Crime Victim's Book.* New York: Basic Books, 1979.

Barkas, J. L. *Victims.* New York: Charles Scribner's Sons, 1978.

Crime in the United States (Uniform Crime Reports). Issued by FBI in annual volumes.

Criminal Victimization in the United States. National Criminal Justice Information and Statistics Services, Annual volumes since 1973.

Drapkin, Israel, and Emilio Viana, editors. *Victimology: A New Focus.* Lexington, MA: D. C. Heath. Five volumes:

Volume 1. *Theoretical Issues in Victimology,* 1974.

Volume 2. *Society's Relationship to Victimization,* 1974.

Volume 3. *Crimes, Victims and Justice,* 1974.

Volume 4. *Violence and Its Victims,* 1975.

Volume 5. *Victimolgy, A New Focus,* 1975.

Goddwin, John. *Murder USA: The Ways We Kill Each Other.* New York: Balantine Books, 1978.

Hentig, Hans von. *The Criminal and His Victim.* New Haven, Connecticut: Yale University Press, 1948.

Hoff, Lee Ann. *People in Crises, Understanding and Helping.* Addison-Wesley Pulishing Company, 1978.

Hudson, Joe, and Burt Galaway. *Considering the Victim.* Springfield, Illinois: Charles C. Thomas, 1975.

————. *Victims, Offenders and Alternative Sanctions.* Lexington, Massachusetts: D. C. Heath, 1980.

Hunt, Morton. *The Mugging.* New York: Atheneum, 1972.

Hyde, Margaret O. *Crime and Justice in Our Time.* New York: Franklin Watts, 1980.

————. *Cry Softly: The Story of Child Abuse.* Philadelphia: Westminster Press, 1980.

————. *Juvenile Justice and Injustice.* New York: Franklin Watts, 1983.

————. *My Friend Wants to Run Away.* New York: McGraw-Hill, 1980.

————. *Speak Out on Rape.* New York: McGraw-Hill, 1976.

MacDonald, John. *Armed Robbery.* Springfield, Illinois: Charles C. Thomas, 1975.

Mandell, Mel. *Being Safe.* New York: Saturday Review Press, 1972.

Nicholson, George; Thomas W. Condit; and Stuart Greenbaum. *Forgotten Victims: An Advocates Anthology.* Sacramento, California: California District Attorneys Association, 1977.

Prescott, Peter S. *The Child Savers.* New York: Alfred A. Knopf, 1981.

Reif, Robert. *The Invisible Victim.* New York: Basic Books, 1979.

Ryan, William. *Blaming the Victim.* New York: Random House, 1976.

Schafer, Stephen. *Victimology: The Victim and His Criminal.* Reston, Virginia: Reston Publishing Company, 1977.

Silberman, Charles E. *Criminal Violence, Criminal Justice.* New York: Random House, 1978.

Toch, Hans H. *Violent Men: An Inquiry Into the Psychology of Violence.* Chicago: Aldine Publishing Company, 1969.

Viano, Emilio, editor. *Victims and Society.* Washington: Visage Press, 1976.

Walker, Lenore. *The Battered Woman.* New York: Harper and Row, 1979.

Wooden, Kenneth. *The Children of Jonestown.* New York: McGraw-Hill, 1981.

———. *Weeping in the Playtime of Others: America's Incarcerated Children.* New York: McGraw-Hill, 1976.

SOURCES OF FURTHER INFORMATION

American Bar Association
Section of Criminal Justice
1800 M Street, N.W.
Washington, D.C. 20036

Child Find, Inc.
P.O. Box 277
New Paltz, New York 12561

Crime Prevention Coalition
Box 6600
Rockville, Maryland 20850

Crime Victims Legal Advocacy Institute
F and M Building, Suite 9
210 Laskin Road
Virginia Beach, Virginia 23451

Criminal Justice and the Elderly
1511 K Street, N.W., Suite 540
Washington, D.C. 20005

*Families and Friends of Missing Persons
and Violent Crime Victims*
P.O. Box 21444
Seattle, Washington 98111

*International Association
of Chiefs of Police*
13 First Field Road
Gaithersburg, Maryland 20878

*National Association for
Crime Victims Rights*
P.O. Box 16161
Portland, Oregon 97216

*National Council on
Crime and Delinquency*
411 Hackensack Avenue
Hackensack, New Jersey 07601

*National Council of Jewish Women
St. Louis Section*
8420 Delmar Boulevard
St. Louis, Missouri 63124

National Crime Prevention Coalition
Box 6700
Rockville, Maryland 20850

*National Criminal Justice
Reference Service*
Box 6000
Rockville, Maryland 20850

*National District Attorneys
Association Commission on
Victim Witness Assistance*
666 North Lake Shore Drive, Suite 1432
Chicago, Illinois 60611

*National Organization for
Victim Assistance*
National Headquarters:
1757 Park Road N.W.
Washington, D.C. 20010

National Sheriffs Association
1250 Connecticut Avenue, N.W.
Washington, D.C. 20036

National Victims of Crime
715 Eighth Avenue S.E.
Washington, D.C. 20003

Parents of Murdered Children
1739 Bella Vista
Cincinnati, Ohio 45237

Superintendent of Documents
U.S. Government Printing Office
Washington, D.C. 20402

Victim Services Agency
For New York Area:
2 Lafayette Street
New York, New York 10007
For other areas, consult phone book.

DIRECTORY OF OFFICES OF STATE CRIME VICTIM COMPENSATION

Violent Crime Compensation Board
Pouch N
Juneau, Alaska 99811

Victims of Crime Program
State Board of Control
926 J Street, Suite 300
Sacramento, California 95814

Victim Compensation Program
80 Washington Street
Hartford, Connecticut 06115

Violent Crime Compensation Board
800 Delaware Avenue, Suite 601
Wilmington, Delaware 19801

Crimes Compensation Commission
2562 Executive Center Circle East
Tallahasee, Florida 32301

Claims Advisory Board
State Capitol Building, Room 214
Atlanta, Georgia 30334

Criminal Injuries Compensation Commission
P.O. Box 399
Honolulu, Hawaii 96809

Crime Victims Program
Department of the Attorney General
188 West Randolf
Chicago, Illinois 60601

Violent Crime Reparations Board
503 Kansas Avenue, Suite 343
Topeka, Kansas 66603

Crime Victims Compensation Board
113 East Third Street
Frankfort, Kentucky 40601

Criminal Injuries Compensation Board
1123 North Eutaw Street
Baltimore, Maryland 40601

Assistant Attorney General
Torts Division
One Ashburton Place
Boston, Massachusetts 02108

Crime Victims Compensation Board
111 S. Capitol Avenue
Lansing, Michigan 48909

Crime Victims Reparations Board
160 East Kellogg Boulevard
St. Paul, Minnesota 55101

Crime Victims Unit
Workmen's Compensation Division
815 Front Street
Helena, Montana 59601

Crime Victims Reparation Board
State Capitol—Sixth Floor
Lincoln, Nebraska 68509

Board of Examiners
209 E. Musser Street, Room 205
Carson City, Nevada 89710

Violent Crimes Compensation Board
1180 Raymond Blvd.
Newark, New Jersey 07102

Crime Victims Compensation Board
270 Broadway
New York, New York 10007

Crime Victims Reparations
Workmen's Compensation Bureau
Russel Building—Highway 83 North
Bismark, North Dakota 58505

Victims of Crime Division Court of Claims
255 East Main Street, 2nd Floor
Columbus, Ohio 43215

Crime Victims Compensation Fund
SAIF Building
Salem, Oregon 97312

Crime Victims Compensation Board
Justice Department
Strawberry Square
Harrisburg, Pennsylvania 17120

Office of State Court Administrator
Providence County Court House
250 Benefit Street
Providence, Rhode Island 02903

Criminal Injuries Compensation Board
State Board of Claims
450 James Robertson Parkway
Nashville, Tennessee 37219

Texas Industrial Accident Board
Crime Victim Division
P.O. Box 12757
Capital Station
Austin, Texas 78701

Division of Crime Victims Compensation
Industrial Commission of Virginia
P.O. Box 1794
Richmond, Virginia 23214

Crime Victims Compensation Commission
P.O. Box 539
St. Thomas, Virgin Island 00801

Crime Victims Division
Department of Labor and Industries
Olympia, Washington 98504

Crime Victims Compensation Bureau
P.O. Box 7951
Madison, Wisconsin 53707

GLOSSARY

Aggravated Assault: a particularly brutal assault; a physical attack with a weapon or one that results in serious bodily injury.

Assault: an intentional threat or attempt to do violent harm to another person.

Battered wives: women who have been beaten or otherwise severely injured by spouses.

Battery: unlawful touching or hurting of another person.

Blood feud: a feud involving blood relatives.

Burglary: breaking and entering with the intent to commit a crime. Differs from robbery, which involves contact with another person.

Capital punishment: imposition of the death penalty by the state.

Child abuse: serious harm to a child that may be physical, emotional, or sexual in nature.

Civil law: that division of law which is concerned with private rights, as opposed to criminal law.

Code of Hammurabi: an ancient and famous code of laws, generally humanitarian, but specific and severe about retribution.

Compensation: an attempt to make amends; recompense; an act which a court orders to be done; equivalent for property taken or for injury done.

Composition: the resolution of differences by an agreement or settlement, usually monetary. In ancient law, a procedure that attempted to "make the victim whole." It might combine compensation and punishment.

Crime of passion: an attack in which the victim is well known to and emotionally involved with the offender.

Criminal justice system: the legal system involved with identifying, determining guilt, sentencing, and punishing of criminal offenders.

Criminal law: the division of law which is concerned with acts of commission or acts for which the state prescribes, in the name of society, a punishment.

Defendant: the person charged with a crime or a tort; the person against whom a plaintiff brings action.

Defense attorney: the lawyer who represents the accused.

District attorney: one who represents the state or government in a criminal case.

Domestic violence: the battering or severely injuring of children, spouses, or parents by family members.

English common law: the principles of law derived through the years and embodied in court decisions, as distinguished from statutory or codified law.

Homicide: the killing of a human being by another.

Incest: sexual relations between persons closely related other than by marriage; usually refers to those who are related biologically but is sometimes considered to include cases of stepparents and children.

"Making the victim whole": an expression used to describe restoring property and emotional health to victims.

Plaintiff: a person who starts a lawsuit.

Precipitation of a crime: the act of bringing about a crime prematurely, hastily, or suddenly; a victim who precipitates a crime does something to cause a crime to happen.

Prosecutor: a person who conducts criminal proceedings on behalf of the state.

Rape: sexual assault upon a person.

Restitution: reimbursement to the victim of a crime for loss or for expenses incurred; often imposed on an offender as a condition of probation.

Retaliation: the act of returning like for like.

Robbery: theft directly from a person by force or threat of force.

Self-victimization: hurting one's self through the use of drugs or weapons; putting one's self in a position that will make one a victim.

Statute: a law duly enacted by a legislature.

Statutory rape: a sexual offense in which the victim is under the age of consent.

Subpoena: an order to appear in court at a certain time to give testimony.

Tort: a civil wrong; the violation of a personal right; a legal wrong done to the property or person of another.

Vandalism: deliberate destruction of property either mischievously or maliciously.

Witness: a person who observes or has knowledge of an event; except in the case of homicide, the crime victim is usually a witness.

Victimologist: one who specializes in the study of victims and those who surround them: witnesses, bystanders, good samaritans, survivors, families, and others.

INDEX

Abused children, 20–21, 43–44, 53

Accused, rights of, 3

Age of criminals and their victims, 7–8

Agencies for services to crime victims, 52, 54, 57–64

Aid for Victims of Crime, Inc., St. Louis, Missouri, 59

Alarm systems, 90–91

Alertness and personal safety, 82–92

Allen, Nancy H., 29

American Bar Association, Criminal Justice Section, 60, 75

Anger of victims, 36–44

Anglo-Saxon England, criminal justice and, 19–20

Assault, victims of, 4, 30, 40–44, 52, 53, 74, 85–89

Assistance for victims of crime, 49–54, 57–64. *See also* Financial assistance for victims of crime

Atlanta, Georgia, murders, 12

Attitudes of society to victims, 4, 10

Awards to victims, compensation, 71–72

Battered women, 20–21, 27–28, 42–43, 52–53

Bill of rights for victims, 72–74

Biologically weak victims, vulnerability of, 31

Blame of victim for offense, 25–27

Blaming the Victim (Ryan), 25

Blood feuds, 15–16

Book of Exodus, 17

Building A Solution: A Practical Guide for Establishing Crime Victim Service Agencies (Susman and Vittert), 54

Buildings, personal safety and, 85

Bureau of Justice Statistics, 5, 9

Bureau of Justice Statistics Bulletins, 9

Burgess, Ann, 42

Cardozo, Benjamin, Supreme Court Justice, 32

Carrington, Frank, 75

Case histories, 6, 7, 10–11, 25, 26–29, 35–36, 37–38, 39, 40–41, 49–51, 57–58, 59–60, 61, 68, 71–72, 74–76, 85, 87

Child abuse, 20–21, 43–44, 53

Classification of victims, 29–32

Code of King Hammurabi, 17–18, 71

Community service by offender as restitution, 68

Compensation, government, for victim of crime, 58, 67, 70–78. *See also* Restitution to victim by offender

Compensation laws, 70–71

"Composition" system of criminal justice, 18–19

Court delays and postponements, 61–63

Court monitors, 74

Crime, hidden costs of, 3

Crime deterrence, 81–92

Crime rate, 5, 8–10

Crime Victims Legal Advocacy Institute, Virginia Beach, Virginia, 75, 76

Criminal justice system, treatment of victim by, 4, 60–64, 67–78; evolution of, 15–21

Criminal-victim relationship, 25–32

Depressed persons, victimization of, 30

Domestic violence, 20–21, 27–28, 42–44, 52–53, 74

Drinkers, victimization of, 8

Early systems of justice, 15–19

Education as means of protecting rights of victim, 76–77
Elderly, victimization of, 11–12, 21, 30, 81. *See also* Case histories
Ellis, Albert, 26
Emotional reactions of victim, 10–12, 35–45; response by society, 49–54, 57–61
Empey, LaMar, 7
Escape attempts, personal safety and, 87–88

Family survivors of murder victim, 53–54
Family violence, 20–21, 27–28, 42–44, 52–53, 74
Fear resulting from crime, 10–12, 36–37, 41, 53
Female murderers, previous abuse of by victims, 27–28
Females, victimization of, 4, 20–21, 27–28, 30, 42–43, 52–53, 81
Financial assistance for victims of crime, 16–20, 58, 67–78
Financial problems of victim, 57. *See also* Case histories
Fines as compensation, 18–20

Fisher, James F., III, 76
Francis, Connie, case history, 75
Funding for victim service agencies, 59, 63

Gamblers, victimization of, 8
Gay, Roxanne, case history, 27
German tribes, criminal justice and, 18–19
Good Samaritan Network, St. Louis, Missouri, 58–59
Government compensation for victim of crime, 58, 67, 70–78. *See also* Restitution to victim by offender
Grayson, Elizabeth, 81
Group retaliation for offense, 15, 16–17
Group support of crime victim, 36–37
Guilt feelings of victim, 39–44

Hammurabi code, 17–18, 71
Hidden victims of crime, 10–11
Hobhouse, L.T., 16
Hofstra University, 81
Homicide: Perspectives on Prevention (Allen), 29

Homicide victim, surviving
family of, 11, 35, 53–54.
See also Case histories
Homosexuals, victimization
of, 8
Homstrom, Linda Lyle, 42
Hostility to crime victims,
51
Hotlines for victims of crime,
58
Howard Johnson Company,
75
Hughes, Francine, case
history, 27–28
Hullinger, Charlotte, 53
Humiliation of victim, 36–44

Identification of attacker,
88–89
Identity and role of victim,
3–12, 19–21, 25–32
Immigrants, victimization
of, 30
Incest, victims of, 43–44
Infrared detectors used in
alarm systems, 90–91
Irrational crime, 5–6

Justice, evolution of, 15–21

Keys, personal safety and, 84

Life-style, vulnerability and, 8

Locking up, personal safety
and, 89–90
Lonely persons,
victimization of, 30

McNamara, Donald, 8
"Making the Victim Whole"
(McNamara and
Sullivan), 8
Mangino case history, 7
Media treatment of crime,
4
Medical attention
for victim of
sexual assault, 53
Medical problems of victim,
53, 57
Mentally retarded,
victimization of, 30
Minorities, victimization of,
30
Mistaken identity, victims
of, 7
Money-handling, personal
safety and, 83–84
Morals in Evolution
(Hobhouse), 16
Mostel, Zero, 25
Mugging, precautions
against, 81–89
Murder victim, surviving
family of, 11, 35, 53–54.
See also Case histories

National Association for
  Crime Victims' Rights, 76
National Council of Jewish
  Women, 54, 58
National Crime Survey, 9, 11
National District Attorneys
  Associaton, 62, 72, 92
National Organization for
  Victim Assistance
  (NOVA), 60, 63, 92
National Victims of Crime,
  5, 92
Neglect, victim's feelings of,
  57, 58
Neighborhood Watch
  programs, 92
New York City Police
  Department, 8
New York State Crime
  Victims Compensation
  Board, 71, 72
New York Times, The, 5, 6
Notification of victims and
  witnesses, 62–64, 72–74

Offense against the state,
  concept of, 20
Office of Juvenile Justice and
  Delinquency Prevention,
  68
Older people, victimization
  of, 11–12, 21, 30, 81. *See
  also* Case histories

Outlawing offender in early
  justice systems, 19–20

Parents of Murdered
  Children, 54
Paris Prison Congress, 1895,
  71
Penalties for assault and
  homicide in early justice
  systems, 17–18
Pennsylvania, University of,
  6
Personal safety, 28–29, 30,
  81–92
Photoelectric beams used in
  alarm systems, 90
Physical coordination,
  vulnerability and, 82
Physical damage inflicted on
  victims, 52
Pius, John, case history,
  6–7, 11
"Pocket operator" burglars,
  90
Political victims, 31–32
Potential victims, 29–32
Precautions against
  becoming a victim, 81–92
Precipitation of crime by
  victim, 27–29
Precipitative victims, 31
Pregnancy as result of rape,
  fear of, 53

Pressure mats used in alarm systems, 90

Prevention programs, crime, 91–92

Promotion of services for victims, 63–64

Prostitutes, victimization of, 8

Provocative victims, 30

Psychological dependence of victims of domestic violence, 42–44

Public education as means of protecting rights of victim, 76–77

Random crime, 5–6

Rape, victims of, 4, 40–42, 53, 74–75

Rape crisis centers, 74

Resisting armed robbery, personal safety and, 28–29

Responding to the feelings of victims, 49–54

Restitution Initiative, 68

Restitution to victim by offender, 16–20, 67–69. *See also* Government compensation of crime victims

Retaliation for offenses, 15, 16, 17–18

Rights of victims, bill of, 72–74

Risk reduction, 28–29, 30, 81–92

Role and identity of victim, 3–12, 19–21, 25–32

Ryan, William, 25

Safety, personal, 28–29, 30, 81–92

Schafer, Stephen, 16, 30

Seattle Community Accountability Board, 69

Security systems, 90–91

Self-defense, personal safety and, 85–88

Self-victimizing victims, 31

Senior citizens, victimization of, 11–12, 21, 30, 81. *See also* Case histories

Service agencies for victims of crime, 52, 54, 57–64

Sexual assault, victims of, 4, 30, 40–44, 53, 74

Sexually abused children, 43–44, 53

Shelters for victims of domestic violence, 74

"Smash and grab" burglars, 90

Snyder v. Massachusetts, 1934, Supreme Court case, 32

Socially weak victims, 31

Southern California, University of, 7

Statistics, crime, 5, 8–10
Street crime, personal safety
  and, 82–84
Sullivan, John H., 8
Support for crime victims,
  49–54
Support of crime prevention
  programs, 91–92
Susman, Marjorie, 54

Temporary insanity plea
  as grounds for acquittal,
  28
Theft, protection against,
  89–91
Third-party suits, 74–76

Ultrasonic devices used in
  alarm systems, 90
United States Supreme
  Court, 32, 76
Unrelated victims, 30
Unreported crimes resulting
  from maltreatment of
  victim, 61
Urban crime, 5, 8
Urban Review, The, 8

Venereal disease resulting
  from rape, fear of, 53
Victim, identity and role of,
  3–12, 19–21, 25–32
Victim-criminal
  relationship, 25–32

Victimology, study of
  victim's role, 4
*Victimology: The Criminal
  and His Victim* (Schafer),
  16, 30
Victim Rights Week, 63
Victim service agencies, 52,
  54, 57–64
Victim Service Agency, New
  York City, 58
Victim Service Council, St.
  Louis, Missouri, 58
Victim Witness Assistance
  Project, American Bar
  Association, 60
Victims Committee,
  American Bar
  Association, 75
Violence, domestic, 20–21,
  27–28, 42–44, 52–53, 74
Violence provoked by
  victim, 27–29
Violent crime, universal need
  of rational explanation
  for, 26
Vittert, Carol Holt, 54
Volunteer training
  programs, 52
Volunteer work with victims,
  54, 58–60
von Hentig, Hans,
  29
Vulnerability to attack,
  81–92

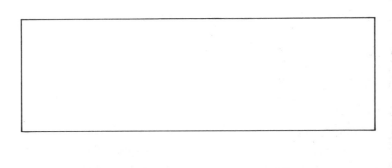

ABOUT THE AUTHOR

Margaret O. Hyde is the author of over forty books for young people, many of them on thought-provoking social issues. Her books for Franklin Watts include *Crime and Justice in Our Time; Juvenile Justice and Injustice* (revised and updated in 1983); *Suicide: The Hidden Epidemic;* and *Foster Care and Adoption.* She has also written several documentary programs for televison.

Margaret Hyde and her husband live in Burlington, Vermont.